THE GREAT GALEOTO AND FOLLY OR SAINTLINESS

THE GREAT GALEOTO
FOLLY OR SAINTLINESS

TWO PLAYS DONE FROM THE VERSE OF

JOSÉ ECHEGARAY

INTO ENGLISH PROSE BY

HANNAH LYNCH

Fredonia Books
Amsterdam, The Netherlands

The Great Galeoto and Folly or Saintliness:
(Two Plays)

by
Jose Echegaray

ISBN: 1-4101-0611-X

Copyright © 2004 by Fredonia Books

Fredonia Books
Amsterdam, The Netherlands
http://www.fredoniabooks.com

All rights reserved, including the right to reproduce this book, or portions thereof, in any form.

In order to make original editions of historical works available to scholars at an economical price, this facsimile of the original edition is reproduced from the best available copy and has been digitally enhanced to improve legibility, but the text remains unaltered to retain historical authenticity.

INTRODUCTION [1]

THE Spanish theatre has for so long been out of fashion that a revived interest in it would carry us into a sort of renaissance. It is not virgin soil, like the drama of the north which has so lately caught the ear of Europe. This, perhaps, accounts for its lack of distinctive originality. For even in Echegaray's notable plays, strong and original as they are, there is an unmistakable ring of the past. We feel it is more a revival than a youthful outburst, with all the promise of novelty. True, it is dominated by the modern need and its restless searching note; it must prove its mission as something more than the mere desire to divert. Not even a sermon could be more remote than this theatre from the old comedy of manners, of loose morals and diverting intrigue, all weighing as lightly on the dramatist's conscience as on the audience's. And it may be questioned if Echegaray, a professor of mathematics as well as a dramatist and poet, could be induced to accept Mr. Stevenson's well-known and not inappropriate classification of the artist as of the family of Daughters of Joy. His is no neutral voice between vice and virtue, concerned solely for the pleasure or

[1] Part of this introduction is reprinted from an article in the *Contemporary Review*, and my thanks are due to the publishers for the permission.

interest of the hour, suing approbation through laughter and wit, or sympathy through dramatic tears. Lest his audience should fail to carry their musings on the problems of life to the theatre in the proper modern spirit, he starts by pricking their conscience and exciting thought that as little relieves them from the pressure of reality as one of Ibsen's plays—though with the latter his having nothing else in common but this determined purpose.

José Echegaray was born at Madrid in 1832. The years of childhood were passed in Murcia, where at the university he studied and took out his degrees. His tendency in youth was towards the exact sciences, with which he still coquets in the same spirit of pride that pushed Goethe to glory in his devotion to painting. He more readily offers to his friends a volume of his *Modern Theories of Physics* or the *Union of Material Forces* by which he is known to a select few, than one of his popular dramas. Of the scientific value of these works I am not in a position to offer any opinion. For career, he chose that of engineer, and, we are told, gave evidence in this line of quite exceptional diligence and quickness. Certain it is that in this department as well as in others that followed, he has amply proved that in individual circumstances the Don may be carried into a permanent frenzy of industry. In 1853 his studies in engineering terminated. Echegaray was appointed successively to posts in various provinces, until he returned to Madrid as professor of the School of Engineers. Here he taught theoretical and applied mathematics, and while building up a serious reputation in science, he found time to study political economy, and devour every form of literature, thus preparing for his future honours as poet and dramatist. He took part in the revolution of 1868, and was appointed Director of Public Works and Minister of Commerce. This post he resigned in 1872, and shortly afterwards that of Minister of Finances, which he was forced to give up on proclamation of the Republic. Then he emigrated to Paris, where he composed his first play *El Libro Talonario*. In 1874 the political situation permitted his return to Spain, and he was nominated Minister for the third time. After that he began to hold himself more and more aloof from public life, and took to writing for the theatre with prodigious activity. Well advanced in middle age, he seems to have taken Lope de Vega for his model in the matter of production. Within twenty years he has written more than fifty plays. In a letter before me, he offers me a choice of his recent plays (whose appearance can only cover a couple of years, I believe), and thus names them off:—*El Critico Incipiente, Los Dos Fanatismos, El Haroldo, El Milagro en Egipto, Siempre en Ridiculo, Sic vos non vobis*, etc. etc., the double etc. suggesting at least half a dozen more, I suppose.

This fatal facility is one of the drawbacks of Spanish talent. The race writes without difficulty, which perhaps is the reason that it writes without finish or distinction. Add to which in adopting French romanticism, upon which wave it was irresistibly carried, it did but accommodate the adoption of the natural bent of its own still mediæval nature. For modern Spanish romanticism belongs more probably to the sixteenth than to the nineteenth century. It is interesting to note the rebound with which Victor Hugo's bell cast this semi-civilised and dreaming people back into their own appropriate century. They prate to-day in Madrid glibly enough of English improvements, clubs, electricity, French vaudevilles, and all the pernicious refinements of our modern civilisation. But these elements are extraneous, a sort of diverting masquerade in their daily life. At heart they are purely mediæval. In all the great moments on and off the stage, they forget the silk hat and coat of civilisation, and walk and talk as if a sword still absurdly cocked the cloak of romance.

In this hour, when foreign Shakespeares are springing up around us with incredible profusion, it would be an agreeable task to come forward with a Spanish Shakespeare. But Don José Echegaray is no such thing. He bears no resemblance to the new geniuses hailed with such delight. He has none of the subtlety of Maeterlinck, and certainly offers entertainment by means of tricks less reminiscent of our start in modern languages. His literary baggage reveals neither the depth nor the flashes of luminous thought with which Ibsen startles us through an obscurity of atmosphere, a childish baldness, and an unconventional disregard of all the old-fashioned theories upon which the laws of dramatic criticism have been formed. But if Echegaray is less original, he is creditably more sane. The lack of depth carries with it a corresponding absence of crudeness and of an artlessness often so bewildering as to leave us imperfectly capable of distinguishing the extreme fineness of the line between genius and insanity. The lucid air of the south clarifies thought, and produces nothing less sober than Latin bombast and the high-phrased moods of the Don.

What is more to be deplored in Echegaray's plays is the absence of French art. An artist in the polished, complete sense he cannot be described. He has none of the French dramatist's incision, none of his delicate irony, his playfulness and humorous depravity, none of his beautiful clarity of expression, still less of his polish, his wit, and consummate dexterity. Poetry is his favourite form of dramatic expression, but it is not the suave measured poetry of M. Richepin; and while he often takes his inspiration from the Middle Ages, he offers us nothing like the ethereal and fanciful verse of M. Armand Silvestre, when that author condescends to forget that he is *fin de siècle*, and seeks to please through the sweetness and delicacy of some mediæval legend. Echegaray is poet enough to delight in these thrilling ages. But his treatment of them generally leaves us cold. It lacks fancy and buoyancy. Sombre passion does not adequately fill the place of absent humour. It is often thin and false, and glaringly artificial, like the mediæval romance of an inefficient author. It is a remarkable fact that such a play as *Mar sin Orillas* (Shoreless Sea) should have achieved popularity in a town so imitatively, not intellectually, modern as Madrid. It has no originality whatever, and offers nothing as compensation for dulness. It is of the Middle Ages, but without the captivating atmosphere of those plumed and belted centuries. It runs complacently along the old dusty highroad; swords clash, knights march off to glory and the Turkish wars, and beauty at home struggles with parental enmity, is sore distraught and belied, and while we are reminded in the high tone of the ancient singers, that

> 'Amor que á la guerra fué
> Sabe Dios si volverá,'

we are confused by the stupidity of everybody.

This repertory is extended, but can hardly be called varied. The one note of undiluted drama runs through all, and while the poet declaims upon a lofty level, it may be said that he chiefly reaches poetry through means of the felicitous vocables of the language he has the privilege to write, rather than by reason of any real genius as a poet. He is concerned more with striking situations than with development or revelation of character. In this line he is totally lacking in diversity and subtlety. He apprehends woman in none other but the crude, mediæval form. To him she is simply a personality of divine and inexhaustible love—an exalted and inalterable ideal; and whether she wears modern raiment or the garb of remote centuries, she is never anything but a spiritualised stain-glass outline, which affords gross and barbaric males—Velasquez' heroes and high-toned villains—much opportunity to rant of saints and angels, and is a subject for continuous worship, ill-treatment, misunderstanding, and devotion to death.

The very titles of these plays have a fine melodramatic ring—*The Avenger's Bride, On the Sword's Point, In the Bosom of Death*, and *Death upon the Lips*, etc. In Spanish the titles are beautiful and inspiring enough to justify choice. *En el Seno de la Muerte* is a particularly impressive play, which rings imagination back into the thirteenth century almost upon a thrill with its strong Hugoesque tinge of romance. There is no fluted fervour of lovers, no thrum of lute or impassioned sequidilla to enliven the roll of solemn wedded passion and betrayal. Remorse and stern hidalgic resentment stalk the stage grandiloquently to the blare of trumpets, royal entrances and exits, and the hum of the Roussillon wars. We have the inevitable struggle between love and duty, the inevitable sombre judgment and full-dress sentiments of virtue. Echegaray has apparently no understanding of vice except as subject for castigation. The bastard Manfred, beloved of his legitimate brother and seignor, loves his sister-in-law Beatrix. Don Jaime, the injured husband, has all the noble and melancholy charm of a Velasquez portrait, the model upon which the dramatist would seem to have drawn his unvarying study of the Middle Ages Don. They all carry their black velvet and plumes with the same high air, seem equally unacquainted with smiles and the lighter emotions, and breathe the same unapproachable perfection in domestic life. For each one the wife is sovereign lady, and if they betray anger, it is the anger of heroes who never forget that they are hidalgoes, and who are incapable of falling, upon any provocation, into triviality or pleasantry of speech. Small blame to the ladies of such lords if they sometimes forget their oath of allegiance, and occasionally decline upon lesser natures. However picturesque, as housemates these Velasquez gentlemen are beyond endurance, and deserve to perish victims of their own relentless nobility.

Don Jaime adored his wife and loved his half-brother. Both in turn loved him, and recognised to the full his claim upon their mutual admiration. But this was naturally no impediment to their own frailty, though not even Echegaray's sinners are for one moment permitted to give a cheerful aspect to sin. It is perhaps a double unwisdom to stoop to folly when they mean to be so persistently miserable over it. Certain it is, that in this case the lady's choice cannot have been prompted by any desire for a lively change. Manfred is only a more scowling, discontented edition of the legitimate Don. 'You are sadder than ever, and your hand avoids the touch of mine,' he complains to Beatrix in the beginning of the second act. And she replies: 'I am ever sad. Sorrow is throned within my bosom, and so imperious is its possession, that death alone can free its slave.' And then when Manfred prays for death as a mutual deliverance, she reproaches him: 'Does my love not then suffice you? If so, live and enjoy it, or confess that of our sin the vase only contains the bitterness, the shame and the disenchantment.'

MANFRED. Your love is but a lie, since I strain in my embrace naught but a cold and inert marble statue. While your soul, your mind, yourself—all that I most fondly love eludes the touch of my lips, and my heart hears the disdainful murmur: 'This is not for the bastard.'

BEATRIX. 'Tis not so. You do not understand me.

MANFRED. Yes, I understand you. You have only loved Jaime.

BEATRIX. So deeply have I loved you, Manfred, that I have forsaken Jaime, noble as he is, for you who are so base. I have given myself to you, drawn by the attraction of the abyss which is your love. And I thought that I could live and be happy under cover of my sin, but it may not be. For ever between my breast and your arms he interposes.

They try to persuade themselves upon insufficient evidence that Jaime is dead, but Beatrix, the more nervous and impressionable of the two, endures the conviction of her senses that her husband lives as the added torture of fear to insistent remorse. Every sound that disturbs the silence, as they sit together by the fire, carries menace of his approach. 'Why are we not happy since we love one another?' Manfred bitterly cries, interrupting her terrified listening. Here is the keynote of Echegaray's philosophy, whether he marshals the dead centuries before us, or treats of the modern conscience. Even in the less complex ages, when the world was younger and fresher, he will not hear of obedience to instinct unpunished before even the fruit has had time to turn to ashes.

We understand that we are commanded to contemplate unrelieved gloom of sentiment and situation upon the entrance of Don Jaime, back from the Roussillon wars in company with Don Pedro, king of Aragon. The guilty lovers have an enemy in one Juana, the duenna and wife of Roger, the squire, who, discovering Beatrix and Manfred in a passionate embrace, is set upon by the infuriated bastard and inadvertently driven upon the sword's point into the family vault, where the door slams upon him with a secret spring. When Manfred has excited the king's anger by scornful rejection of the favour of a name and title that shall give him equality with his brother, we realise that the hour is a favourable one for Juana's accusation. Whatever rights a sovereign may arrogate to himself in the matter of his own morals, he is usually a keen arbitrator of the limitations of those of his subjects. On this principle, Don Pedro shows himself merciless to the sinners, though one happens to be his hostess and the other his host's much-loved brother. A rational man would have preferred to blink and turn away, with the safe conclusion that it was, after all, none of his business. But monarchs are allowed so many other attributes, that even out of Spain they may be fitly dispensed with reason. In an interview with the culprits, when a saner man would have been touched with the generous strife between them as to which should bear the blame and punishment, he decides that both shall die. Upon Manfred's petition, he consents that Jaime shall live in ignorance of his wrong, but the poor fool, for all his crown, was not sufficiently master of events to contrive this rash promise. Spanish history may furnish a precedent of such a situation, but we are not taught that the lives of the monarchs of the land explain it adequately. When Jaime enters and remonstrates with Don Pedro:—'I am her owner, sir. All your power, your crown, your greatness, the glory of Sicily and of the entire world—what are they against Beatrix! But smoke and dust,'—the king commutes her sentence to perpetual imprisonment, and orders the execution of Manfred in Barcelona. Upon this Jaime threatens to carry both away with him, forswear his king and country, and cross the frontier. A violent quarrel ensues between him and the king, and in the midst of recriminations, Don Pedro casts his dishonour in the teeth of his angry subject. The unfortunate nobleman, dazed and incredulous, reads Roger's letter, given him by Don Pedro, and falls into a spiritless despair. He asks his sovereign's pardon, and they part reconciled friends. Left alone by the family vault at night, he bursts into a sonorous soliloquy. We remember a somewhat similar situation in Victor Hugo, and are irritated by the reminiscence. There is a natural note in his simple cry to Beatrix to speak to him before she dies—to lie, feign, accuse him,—only speak. Also in the speech to Manfred that follows, when he recalls the time they were playmates together, and then tells bitterly the roll of his wrongs: 'It were kinder to kill me at once,' Manfred cries impetuously. By a curious ineffectuality, a lack of skill, it however falls just short of real pathos. Echegaray is never simple enough to reach pathos. The climax has a false ring. Manfred dies by his own hand, and, following his example, Jaime stabs himself, and falls near him, in the shadow of the tomb.

D. JAIME. Manfred, too, lies dead, and you shortly will follow us. When you die, where will you fall?

BEATRIX. By your side.

D. JAIME. Then come closer—'tis no lie? Answer. [*Clasps her.*]

BEATRIX. No.

D. JAIME. And where will your tears flow?

BEATRIX. Over your body.

D. JAIME. Then see. You must embrace my inert body. Do not cease weeping—so that—thus we drop into the bosom of death.

Death on his Lips takes us into quite another atmosphere. We are in foreign lands, on the distant shore of Lake Geneva, in the heart of the Calvinist Inquisition. The Don is introduced, but only as an exile, in the person of Miguel Servet, a famous Aragonese doctor who was martyred at Geneva in 1553. The Calvinists are painted in befitting blackness by a Spaniard, naturally glad of an opportunity to show that other lands had their Inquisition as well as Spain, and cruelty in those days was to be found as fierce elsewhere. It is a gloomy, a powerful, but not a very interesting play. Servet is well contrasted with the Genevese, the heaviness of the one race being dexterously made to appear so much less amiable and well-mannered than that of the other. The heroine, Margarita (naturally), is the usual heroine of Echegaray's choice—all heart, devotion, generosity, sincerity, and a certain broad intelligence. He may be trusted not to choose a fool, though he may never aspire to striking originality in his portrayal of what he evidently regards as the angelic sex.

On the Sword's Point attains a higher level of dramatic thought. Doña Violante is married to Don Rodrigo—the inevitable Velasquez, in plumes and black velvet. In the first bloom of youth, a titled blackguard had surprised and dishonoured her, and Fernando, her son, is the unsuspected offspring of this shame. He is a fine-spirited young fellow, more fiery and blusterous than the implacably dignified Rodrigo. He loves, and is beloved by, Laura, the ward of his parents. An unconscious vein of humour runs through the pompous scene, in which he is found by these latter on his knees before the girl. Don Rodrigo is shocked at such indelicate boldness—just like the amusing Marquis in *The Sorcerer*. 'They love each other,' Doña Violante expostulates. 'It is necessary to be severe with youth,' the Don replies, repressing his indignation at the bidding of his wife. Then he proceeds to point out to Fernando that henceforth Laura's honour must be as dear to him as his own, and after an eulogy on the virtue of the ladies of his house, he explains that if the stain of dishonour dimmed the splendour of the name of Moncada in a woman, it would be the duty of her husband, father, or brother to kill her on the spot. This is not lively talk for Doña Violante, but life was not a lively matter for women in those dull days—especially in Spain, where it still is the reverse of exciting for them. The young man's ardent youth puzzles Don Rodrigo, it is so unlike his own, and these perplexities are disturbed by the titled blackguard's sudden claim to Laura's hand—whom he describes as a mixture of Turkish houri and Christian virgin. Thereupon ensues a painful scene between the victim and the wrong-doer. The titled blackguard shows himself susceptible of the feelings of a gentleman, and deplores the sin of his rash youth—does he also not wear black velvet and a plumed cap? However, he has no mind to renounce his claim to Laura's hand though Doña Violante kneel to him, and Fernando swagger about with unsheathed steel. The duenna and the squire (from whom a little humour might not unreasonably be expected if it were possible to convict so serious a philosopher as the author with anything like deliberate pleasantry) contrive to muddle the carriage of Doña Violante's passionate letter to her betrayer, speaking of the fatal night with lamentable lucidity, so that it falls into Fernando's hands, who instantly believes that Laura is the injured woman. Some spirited scenes ensue, and Fernando interrupts an interview in the dark as he believes between Laura and his rival. A light reveals his mother's shame, and when Don Rodrigo enters after Laura he does not hesitate to sacrifice himself and the beloved by letting it appear that it was Laura he discovered at a clandestine meeting instead of his mother. The result is that Laura is condemned by the relentless Moncada to marry the titled blackguard, being now too damaged an article for the son of his house. This is a delicate dilemma for a youth with such traditions to live up to: to have to choose between his mother's death and dishonour and the dishonour and loss of his bride. His birth is only revealed to him by Doña Violante to prevent the sacrilegious duel between him and his father, and to guard the dreadful secret Fernando stabs himself. 'My death, mother, blots out your dishonour.' The third act hurries on through many strong effects, and the young man's death we feel to have the appropriate majesty of the inevitable. The situation is so poignant that there could be no other solution, and even the titled blackguard wins our sympathy in that last tragic scene.

The same gloom and power pervade *The Avenger's Bride*, the old story of Montague and Capulet. But here the young Montague, one Don Carlos, slays the traditional family enemy, who happens to be the father of a weak-sighted maiden. She emerges into the strong sunlight just in time to recognise her father's assassin, and then is struck blind. Don Carlos woos her under another name, and an old lover, who is an enlightened oculist of the Middle Ages, restores her sight. Her lover Lorenzo had promised to kill the man she should name her father's murderer. When she cries out, 'Don Carlos,' he keeps his word, and she falls upon his corpse 'the avenger's bride.'

What touches us more closely is Echegaray's manipulation of the modern conscience, and its illimitable scope for reflection, for conflict, and the many-sided drama of temptation. This is familiar ground, and we are ever pleased to welcome a new combatant. That the Spanish dramatist brings a novel note may be accepted after reading the curious prologue to his *Gran Galeoto*. It is the best and most popular of Echegaray's plays. In its printed form it is dedicated to *Everybody*, which is the crowning insistance on the *motif* of the prologue, and there is an introduction by Señor Ignacio José Escobar from which I copy an interesting statement.

'And then came that unforgetable night the 19th March 1881, the night of the first representation of *The Great Galeoto*. There was neither strife nor contradiction, nothing but a universal concert of congratulation, praise, and applause. Here your treatment of a great social problem had the good fortune to run on lines that in all eyes seemed elevated and humane. What a splendid and legitimate satisfaction for those among us who had hesitated to share the general opinion!'

The *Epoca* wrote next day:—'Don José Echegaray has obtained an indisputable, an unanimous triumph. He has treated a great social question in a masterly manner. The great Galeoto felt the rod of shame upon its cheek, but it applauded without a single exception. The social vice exists, we know, and that vice was whipped with all the vigorous energy of a Greek tragedy. Everybody recognised the truth of the picture, though none cared to accept it as personal: but the social moral avenged by the creative genius of Señor Echegaray owes him a reward and satisfaction, and that reward and that satisfaction will be the union of all classes, those who may have once in a way formed part of the great Galeoto, and those who habitually protest against the facile habit of slander—to show their gratitude to the poet, the one for vengeance, and the other for the lesson received.

'A subscription not to exceed twenty reals (four shillings), which will be devoted to some work of art, will recall to Señor Echegaray while he lives that he may obtain triumphs as great as last night's, seeking his inspiration in the true sentiment of art.'

To the extraordinary and self-conscious prelude of *The Great Galeoto* which lifts a play quite out of the region of diversion, and, as the sensible Don Julian remarks, plunges us into philosophy, the written, not acted, prologue to *El Hijo de Don Juan* (Don Juan's Son) may be added as an excellent interpretation of Echegaray's personality, revealed already with passable clearness in the dramatic prologue quoted. He enumerates the conclusions of the critics. That the play was inspired by Ibsen's celebrated *Ghosts*. That the passions it deals with are more appropriate to Northern climes than to the South. That it treats of the problem of hereditary madness. That it discusses the law of heredity. That it is gloomy and lugubrious, with no other object than that of inspiring horror. That it is a purely pathological drama. That it contains nothing but the process of madness. That from the moment it is understood that Lázaro will go mad, all interest in the work ceases, and there remains nothing but to follow step by step the shipwreck of enfeebled intelligence. And so on. Echegaray regards all this as the lamentable exercise of dramatic criticism. The underlying thought of his work is different, but he declines to enter into further explanation of it, each scene and each phrase sufficiently explaining it already. To touch more closely upon the matter would be perilous. Besides, he adds, it is not his habit to defend his plays. Once written, he casts them to their fate, without material or moral defence, and the critics are free to tear themselves to pieces over them. There is one phrase alone that he defends energetically, because it is borrowed from Ibsen, and appears to him of singular beauty: 'Mother, give me the sun.' This he describes in his prologue as 'simple, infantile, half comical, but enfolding a world of ideas, an ocean of feeling, a hell of sorrows, a cruel lesson, the supreme watchword of society —of the family.' He continues, quite in the modern spirit:

'A generation consumed by vice, which carries in its marrow the venom of impure love, in whose corrupted blood the red globules are mixed with putrid matter, must ever fall by degrees into the abysm of idiocy. Lázaro's cry is the last glimmer of a reason dropping into the eternal darkness of imbecility. At that very hour Nature awakes, and the sun rises; it is another twilight that will soon be all light.

'Both twilights meet, cross, salute in recognition of eternal farewell, at the end of the drama. Reason, departing, is held in the grip of corrupting pleasure. The sun, rising, with its immortal call, is pushed forward by the sublime force of Nature.

'Down with human reason, at the point of extinction: hail to the sun that starts another day! 'Give me the sun,' Lázaro cries to his mother. Don Juan also begs it through the tresses of the girl of Tarifa.

'On this subject there is much to be said; it provokes much reflection. If indeed our society—but what the deuce am I doing with philosophy? Let each one solve the problem as best he can, and ask for the sun, the horns of the moon, or whatever takes his fancy. And if nobody is interested in the matter, it only proves that the modern Don Juan has engendered many children without Lázaro's talent.

'Respectful salutations to the children of Don Juan.'

From all this it will be understood that Echegaray presses into the service of pleasure the desperate problems of our natural history, and instead of laughter confronts us with mournful gravity; asks us to stand aghast at inherited injustice, and to doubt with him the wisdom of Providence at sight of such undiminished and idle wickedness in man, and such an accumulation of unmerited suffering. Now-a-days we are inordinately engrossed by such issues, and life weighs more heavily upon our shoulders than it did upon our fathers. The good old spirit of fun is fast being trodden out of us by the pervading sense of a mission, and the laborious duty of converting somebody to something. We no longer go to the theatre to weep over fictitious wrongs and smile at imaginary joys. We go to study what we are pleased to call life; to sip at the founts of philosophy, to hear a sermon. It is not exhilarating, but we thankfully take the draught of wisdom offered us, and go our ways without a murmur that we have been depressed rather than entertained. Cervantes, with old-fashioned sanity of judgment, condemned the practice of preaching sermons through the veil of fiction. What sort of reflection would the pathological novel and drama inspire in so wise and witty an author? He might be led to create a type of character even more mad than the Knight Errant.

El Hijo de Don Juan (Don Juan's Son) is an infinitely crueller and more disagreeable play than *Ghosts* because it is more lucid, more direct. The characters themselves are more carefully drawn, and we have a closer actual acquaintance with them. Here there is not one victim only, but two. Don Juan, the middle-aged *roué*, has a friend, also a middle-aged *roué*. The daughter of his friend, Carmen, is consumptive, and is betrothed to his son, Lázaro, who is subject to vertigo. The play opens with three elderly *roués*, all ill-preserved after a life of scandal, holding converse the reverse of edifying over tobacco and alcohol. Here Echegaray shows how little he means to mince matters by the remarks he puts into the mouth of one of them in reply to Don Juan's boast that the genius of his son is inherited from him. Paternal inheritance would be nothing but rheum or neurosis—'the sediment of pleasure and the residuum of alcohol.' Upon this Don Juan launches into poetry and describes the single moment in which his soul soared above material enjoyments and sighed for the glorious and impossible. It was after an orgy, and as his half-closed eyes saw the sun rise over the Guadalquivir through the silky waves of a girl's hair, he understood the beauty of poetry and Nature, and stretched out a hand to clutch the splendid orb. This desire is afterwards recalled to him in a moment of surprising horror, when his brilliant and beloved son, sinking into imbecility, sees the rising sun, and cries: 'How lovely! Mother, give me the sun.' 'And I also wanted it once,' Don Juan exclaims: 'My God! my son! Lázaro!'

Don Juan, as might be inferred from his name, carries on intrigues with ballet-girls and servant-maids under the nose of his wife and son. Lázaro seems blind enough to parental delinquencies. Not, as he explains himself when complaining of broken health, that he has been a saint because he has eschewed excesses. The scene where he first appears ailing and stupid is singularly painful, above all, towards the end, when, after an outburst of lucid eloquence, he falls drowsily upon the sofa, and feeling sleep upon him, begs that Carmen, his betrothed, should not be permitted to see him in a ridiculous attitude.

XAVIER. Unless you are as beautiful as Endymion she shall not enter. [*Pause. Xavier walks about; Lázaro begins to sleep.*]

LÁZARO. Xavier, Xavier!

XAVIER. What?
LÁZARO. Now I am—half asleep—how do I look?
XAVIER. Very poetical.
LÁZARO. Good. Thanks—very poetical. [*Dreamily.*]

The second act is somewhat livelier, and contains more spirited contrasts. That Echegaray could excel in lighter comedy may be seen in an amusing scene between the serious son and the dissipated, good-natured father.

Don Juan is alone with his son, who is walking restlessly about. The father asks his son what he is thinking of, and then apologises for disturbing weighty thought. Lázaro listlessly replies that his imagination was wandering, and he wandering after it. When he has received many assurances of not being in the poet's way, Don Juan calls for sherry, the Parisian newspapers, and *Nana*. Caught laughing over *Nana*, he asserts his horror of immoral books, and his conviction that literature is going to the dogs.

LÁZARO. Zola is a great writer. Ah, I've caught the idea I was seeking. [*Sits down to write.*]

There is here a little humorous by-play between the servant and Don Juan, and afterwards a reference to the lugubrious theme in converse between her and Lázaro, whose listlessness, courtesy and musing, make an admirable relief against the alert and fussy affection and frivolity of his father.

DON JUAN. Ha, ha! witty, exceedingly witty. Full of salt; hot as red pepper. *Gil Blas* is the only paper worth reading.
LÁZARO. An interesting article? What is it about? Let me see.

DON JUAN. [*Hastily ramming the paper into his pocket.*] A dull and shocking article. I must take it away, for the mischief would be in it if it fell into Carmen's hands.

LÁZARO. You are quite right. [*Beginning to walk again.*]

DON JUAN. I hadn't finished it. I must finish it later. [*Takes up 'Nana.'*] Stupendous! Monumental enough to make one die of laughing. Lord! why do we read but for amusement's sake? Then give us diverting books. [*Laughing.*]

LÁZARO. Is it a witty book?

DON JUAN. [*In altered voice.*] Perhaps. But this light literature soon wearies. [*Seeing Lázaro approach, he hides 'Nana' in another pocket.*] Have you anything substantial to read—really substantial?

LÁZARO. [*Looking through his books.*] Do you like Kant?

DON JUAN. Kant? Do you say Kant? The very thing. He was always my favourite author. When I was young I fell asleep every night over Kant. [*Aside.*] Who the deuce is he?

LÁZARO. If you like I will—— [*Looking for a passage.*]

DON JUAN. No, my son. Any part will do, if it can be read in divisions. Let me see. Don't trouble about me. Write, my son, write. [*Lázaro begins to write, and Don Juan reads.*] 'Beneath the aspect of relation, third moment of taste, the beautiful appears to us the final form of an object, without semblance to finality.' The Devil! [*Holding book away and contemplating it in terror.*] The devil! 'Or as a finality without end.' There are people who understand this! 'Since it is called the final form to the causality of any conception with relation to the object.' Let me see [*holding book still further off*]; 'final form to the causality.' 'Pon my word, I'm perspiring. [*Wipes his forehead.*] 'Conscience is this finality without end, is the play of the cognitive forces.' What! 'The play of cognitive . . . the play' . . . If it were play I should understand it. 'Conscience of this internal causality is what constitutes æsthetic pleasure.' If I continue I shall have congestion. Jesus, Mary, and Joseph! Only think that Lázaro understands the finality without end, the causality and the play of the cognitive forces. Heavens! what a fellow! [*Reads again.*] 'The principle of the methodical conformity of nature is the transcendental principle of the strength of judgment.' [*Strikes the table.*] I should lose myself if I read more. But what a fellow, who can read such stuff and keep sane!

LÁZARO. Does it interest you?

DON JUAN. Immensely. What depth! [*Aside.*] I am five minutes falling into it and haven't yet reached the bottom. I should think it did interest me indeed. But, frankly, I prefer——

LÁZARO. Hegel?

DON JUAN. Just so (*Nana*).

After talk of Lázaro's health and engagement, Don Juan, learning that the young man is pensive or pre-occupied, solely because he is projecting a drama, says he will leave him to thought. Glancing into Kant, he mutters, 'The—the—cognitive forces—the—the—finality, —yes, the finality.' 'Work, my son, work. Above all, write nothing immoral.' He drinks off a glass of sherry, and regretfully remarks that this finality has an end; then marches away with the bottle, *Gil Blas*, and *Nana* to study in solitude.

This is the sole touch of comedy in a play of ever increasing gloom, pervaded by the stupor of the hero and the cough of the heroine. 'My father loves me dearly,

Carmen remarks to Dolores, Don Juan's embittered wife. 'Then he ought to have given you stronger lungs,' the elder woman retorts, with shocking directness. It is indeed, as Echegaray complains the critics assert, a pathological drama. When his friends are not discussing the symptoms of Lázaro's strange malady, he himself is enumerating them in merciless monologues. He talks of his greatness, of his fame, of the popularity of his works, and then falls into childish drivel and longs for playthings. 'His head is not firm,' says Don Nemesis to Carmen's father, in dubiety before the prospect of the marriage; 'that is why he is so stupendous at times, and all the world calls him a genius. Put no trust in geniuses, Timotheus. A genius may walk down one street, and hear the people cry, "The genius!" Let him round the corner into another street, and he will hear the street arab shout after him, "The lunatic!" Much talent is decidedly a dangerous thing.' 'God defend us from it!' piously exclaims the elderly *roué*. 'I have always been very careful not to cultivate it.'

It would be difficult to conceive a more needlessly disagreeable scene than the interview between the celebrated brain doctor and Lázaro, who, the night before, has been consulted by Dolores on behalf of a nephew, and innocently, but with terrible frankness, discusses the case with the unfortunate victim himself. 'We cannot with impunity corrupt the sources of life,' says Doctor Bermúdez, in the high scientific manner, without noticing the increasing emotion of his companion; 'the son of such a father must soon fall into madness or idiocy.' 'Ah! No!

What? My father! I—It is a lie!' Lázaro burst out, in frantic horror. When the poor mother enters the scene and brings her maternal note of despair to the son's distracted terror, we feel that the modern drama has reached a pitch of tragedy unapprehended in healthier and more barbaric ages. 'Lose one's brains as one might lose a hat!' exclaims Don Juan when enlightened. 'Bah! idiots are born so . . . . but a man of genius! . . . Lázaro, who understands *the finality without end* as he knows the *Paternoster*!'

DOLORES. [*Despairingly*.] But if it were true? If it were true? And then? Oh! why was I born? [*Approaching Don Juan who retreats*.] Through you have I lost my illusions, stained my youth, debased my life, forfeited my dignity—through you! And after twenty years of sacrifices, to be worthy of Lazáro! . . . good for his sake, loyal for him, resigned for him, honourable for him, and to-day! . . . No, you have always been a scoundrel; but for once you must be right. Impossible! impossible! God could not will it.

DON JUAN. Good, I have always been a scoundrel. What more? But don't remember it now; above all, don't say it. Say that you forgive me. Forgive me, Dolores.

DOLORES. What does it matter?

DON JUAN. It matters to us both. If you should not forgive me, and if God should remember to punish me, and punish me through my Lázaro!

Pitiful is the poor mother's wavering between softness and bitterness. At one moment she pardons him with all her heart, or only bargains that he shall help her to save their boy. And then when he vows to do so with his whole soul and the remainder of his life, she retorts cruelly,

'With what life you have left; what Heaven, in its mercy, still grants you.' 'Dolores!' the poor wretch exclaims, and again she softens: 'It is true; I had forgiven you.' Upon this the elderly scapegoat brightens and mentions Paris, Germany, England—'the English know so much. Bah! there is a good deal of science scattered over the world.' 'Then let us gather it all for Lázaro.'

This desperate situation is relieved by the entrance of Carmen's father in the black of etiquette, strictly solemn as befits a Spanish father offering his daughter in marriage to his old chum. He says reprovingly: 'Do not embrace me. Don't you see that I am all in black—in the garb of etiquette? It is a very solemn occasion. Call everybody except Lázaro—him later. Solemnity above all.' The afflicted parents have decided to conceal Lázaro's calamity from the world, and make a heart-broken effort to welcome the betrothal with delight, and the gloom of the situation is deepened by the young man's miserable behaviour when called to his beloved.

LÁZARO. Carmen! Mine, mine! I may take her, clasp her in my arms! inflame her with my breath! drink her with my eyes! I may if I like!

DON JUAN. Yes, yes, but enough.

LÁZARO. What infamy! What treason! Carmen!

CARMEN. [*Running to him.*] Lázaro!

LÁZARO. Go, away! Why do you come to me? You cannot be mine. Never, never, never.

CARMEN. Do you give me up? Ah, I have already felt it. Mother! [*Takes refuge in his mother's arms.*]

Nobody understands. Carmen's father is indignant.

Lázaro's confidential friend asks if he has gone mad, and Lázaro, bewildered, turns despairingly to Don Juan: 'Father, father. You are my father. Save me.' 'With my life, my son.' 'You gave me life, but it is not enough. Give me life to live, to love, to be happy. Give me life for Carmen's sake. Give me more life, or cursed be that which you have given me.'

The third act is rendered more sombre if possible from the shabby chatter and airs of aged rake on the part of Carmen's father, with which it starts. We are introduced to the Tarifa girl, Don Juan's old mistress, now pensioned and respectably established on his estate on the banks of the Guadalquivir. Deeper and deeper are we forced to wade through unrelenting shadow. Now it is the frivolous Don Timoteo, sipping his manzanilla, and sneering at the young generation as personated by his daughter Carmen, Lázaro, and Lázaro's friend, the girl with her affected lungs, Lázaro with his dementia, and his friend formal and headachy. 'Ah, in my day we were other,' he sighs. 'Perhaps,' retorts the friend, 'it is because you were—*other* then that we are so now.' Then it is Lázaro, rough, distrustful, and sly, completely altered, afraid to sleep because he does not know how it might be upon his awakening or if he should ever awake, with swift leaps from childish drivel into the Don's plumed phrases, forgetful of modern raiment, and swaggering through imagery and sonorous syllables as if a sword clanked by his side and he carried the spurs of chivalry. And then the poor victim falls to drinking with his father's old mistress, and when half-drunk and wholly mad, plots with her to carry off Carmen.

When she cries out that 'farewell' means tears, he exclaims inconsequently: 'Then you, too, will cry. We will all cry . . . Laughing fatigues, crying rests.'

Quite gay and reckless, he faces Carmen to propose elopement to her. He laments the former coldness of his words and moods, the insufficiency of the vulgar tongue to express passion so burning and impetuous as his, and terrifies her by his wild and flowery volubility. There is night all around him except for the ray of intense light that encircles her face. On that he concentrates all that remains to him of life, of manhood, of feeling, thought and love. He descends from this into weak complaining. Her happiness is threatened by inimical conspiracies, and yet how is he to defend her? He fancies he is in a desert full of sand, plagued with unquenchable thirst and menaced by a falling heaven. He mixes up in the dreariest way the sands of the desert and the old applause that greeted his genius, wonders if either will have an end, then doubts the end of anything, and implores Carmen to save him. 'Help me. Look at me, speak, laugh, cry, do something, Carmen, to keep me from wandering into the desert.' But already his look is vague, and he has ceased to see her. In vain she cries to him that she is near, weeps over him, holds him to her. 'I am Carmen, look at me. The little head you were wont to love so is close to your lips. I am smiling at you. Laugh, Lázaro, answer me. Wake up! Surely you hear me, you see me!' When his mother comes in response to the girl's agonised cry, a glimmer of intelligence gives a sort of dignity to his incoherent words. He wants his mother to console him, for he has to say 'a long, a sad, and solemn farewell to Carmen.' The girl protests she will not leave him, when he irritably orders her away—a great way off. He loved her much, but now it is adieu eternally. He only wishes now to be alone with his parents, until memory suddenly carries him back into the time of quarrel, reproaches, and jealousies of those two in his childhood. 'Don't contradict me, father; you used to quarrel and make me afraid.' He passionately orders him away, too, with Carmen, and turns for comfort to his mother. Then he remembers his school troubles, how his mother coldly parted with him, and to guard against complete loneliness, calls for Paca, his father's old mistress. 'Come, I am young and wish to live,' he cries, and when we find Don Juan aroused to indignation and threatening to fling the Tarifa girl over the balcony into the river if she does not instantly retire, we are ready to hail the mercifulness of Ibsen. This is to carry a sermon to an intolerable length, and drive us so out of love with both philosophy and science as to paint unreason with a double allurement. A father kneeling to his mad son to let an old mistress go, and the son, struggling out of the gathering torpor of intelligence to stare at the rising sun :—

'Mother, how lovely!'
'Lázaro!'
'So lovely! Mother, so lovely! Give me the sun.'
'My God! I also wanted it once,'

sobs Don Juan.

'For ever!'

is the last lugubrious note of Dr. Bermúdez.

It is a relief to turn from this ghastly tragedy to the brighter movement of *El Gran Galeoto*. My printed copy of this play shows it to have run to the twentieth edition, which, for an unreading land like Spain, is an enormous sale. Bright is perhaps a misleading term, for the whole is tinged with the profound melancholy that strikes us in the Spanish gaze, in its character and in the tristful note of its popular songs and dances. The English are supposed to take their pleasures sadly. The saying were more appropriate to the rather dreary race beyond the Pyrenees. Whatever may be their preoccupation (generally speaking it is dulness or an empty mind they are afflicted with rather than sadness) they give the foreigner the impression of being the wholesale victims of a shattered organ which we have the habit of associating with the affections.

In these two dramas—*Don Juan's Son* and *The Great Galeoto*—enough will be understood of the passion of gravity with which the Spanish dramatist enters into the obscurer and less picturesque tragedies of life. Love with him is not the sentimental sighing of maids and boys, as he again shows in *Lo Sublime en lo Vulgar*, but the great perplexed question of married infelicity and misunderstanding. Don Julian dies broken-hearted and wilfully deceived, and his deception it is that forges the tempered happiness of his rival. In *Lo Sublime en lo Vulgar* we have two diverse husbands: Richard, an airy social success, full of elegant phrases, befittingly tailored, and of manners the best—the sort of man destined to float to the surface in all circumstances, and minuet with grace round the ugliest corner. Bernard, whom he betrays and laughs at, is the commonplace, scarce presentable husband, married by a refined and poetical creature for his money, and blushed for by her at every moment while she is solacing herself with the elegant improprieties of her friend's husband, Richard. Here we have another picture of marital jealousy, justifiable in this case, and perhaps for that reason more merciful. Instead of turning from his faithless wife, the insignificant and vulgar Bernard wins her to him and to atonement by an unpretentious magnanimity, and the play ends hopefully with Richard's cry to his wife: 'Louisa, pardon!—and forget!' And Bernard, turning to Inez, his wife, explains his generosity in sonorous verse: 'Honour goes from the soul into the depth, and in the world I put no trust. Since my honour is my own, I understand it infinitely better than the world.'

Not even Tolstoi, with all that delicacy and keenness of the Russian conscience, that profound seriousness, which move us so variously in his great books, has a nobler consciousness of the dignity of suffering and virtue than this Spanish dramatist. And not less capable is he of a jesting survey of life. Echegaray writes in no fever of passion, and wastes no talent on the niceties of art. The morality and discontent that float from the meditative North have reached him in his home of sunshine and easy emotions, and his work is pervaded nobly by its spirit. And unlike Ibsen, he illuminates thought with sane and connected action. Discontent never leads him to the verge of extravagance. Extravagance he conceives to be a part of youth, addicted to bombast and wild words. Man trades in other material than romantic language and rhodomontade. Hence he brings emphasis and plain speech to bear upon him when youth has had its fill through the long-winded, high-coloured phrases of his scribbling heroes. Thought, perhaps, travels too persistently along the shadowed paths, and we should be thankful to find our world reflected through his strong glass, dappled with a little of the uncertain but lovely sunshine that plays not the least part in the April weather of our life here.

The note of unwavering sadness depresses. But, at least, it is not ignoble, and he conceives it borne with so much resignation and dignity that if the picture carries with it the colours of frailty, it brings a counterbalancing conception of the inherent greatness of man.

HANNAH LYNCH.

THE GREAT GALEOTO
A PLAY IN THREE ACTS
WITH A PROLOGUE

PERSONS OF THE DRAMA

TEODORA, Wife of

DON JULIAN.

DONA MERCEDES, Wife of

DON SEVERO.

PEPITO, Their Son.

ERNEST.

A WITNESS.

TWO SERVANTS.

SCENE—*Madrid of our day*.

PROLOGUE

A study; to the left a balcony, on right a door; in the middle a table strewn with papers and books, and a lighted lamp upon it. Towards the right a sofa. Night.

SCENE I

ERNEST. [*Seated at table and preparing to write.*] Nothing—impossible! It is striving with the impossible. The idea is there; my head is fevered with it; I feel it. At moments an inward light illuminates it, and I see it. I see it in its floating form, vaguely outlined, and suddenly a secret voice seems to animate it, and I hear sounds of sorrow, sonorous sighs, shouts of sardonic laughter . . . a whole world of passions alive and struggling. . . . They burst forth from me, extend around me, and the air is full of them. Then, then I say to myself: ''Tis now the moment.' I take up my pen, stare into space, listen attentively, restraining my very heart-beats, and bend over the paper. . . . Ah, but the irony of impotency! The outlines become blurred, the vision fades, the cries and sighs faint away . . . and nothingness, nothingness encircles me. . . . The monotony of empty space, of inert thought, of dreamy lassitude! and more than all the monotony of an idle pen and lifeless paper that lacks the life of thought! Ah! How varied are the shapes of nothingness, and how, in its dark and silent way, it mocks creatures of my stamp! So many, many forms! Canvas without colour, bits of marble without shape, confused noise of chaotic vibrations. But nothing more irritating, more insolent, meaner than this insolent pen of mine [*throws it away*], nothing worse than this white sheet of paper. Oh, if I cannot fill it, at least I may destroy it—vile accomplice of my ambition and my eternal humiliation. Thus, thus . . . smaller and still smaller. [*Tears up paper. Pauses.*] And then! How lucky that nobody saw me! For in truth such fury is absurd and unjust. No, I will not yield. I will think and think, until either I have conquered or am crushed. No, I will not give up. Let me see, let me see . . . if in that way——

SCENE II

Ernest. Don Julian on the right, in evening-dress, with overcoat upon his arm.

D. JULIAN. [*At the door, without entering.*] I say, Ernest!

ERNEST. Don Julian!

D. JULIAN. Still working? Do I disturb you?

ERNEST. [*Rising.*] Disturb me! What a question, Don Julian! Come in, come in. And Teodora?

[*Don Julian enters.*]

D. JULIAN. We have just come from the Opera. She has gone upstairs with my brother, to see something or other that Mercedes has bought, and I was on my way to my room when I saw your light, so I stopped to say good-night.

ERNEST. Was there a good house?

D. JULIAN. As usual. All our friends inquired after you. They wondered you were not there too.

ERNEST. That was kind of them.

D. JULIAN. Not more than you deserve. And how have

you improved the shining hours of solitude and inspiration!

ERNEST. Solitude, yes; inspiration, no. It shuns me though I call on it never so humbly and fondly.

D. JULIAN. It has failed at the rendezvous?

ERNEST. And not for the first time, either. But if I have done nothing else, at least I have made a happy discovery.

D. JULIAN. What?

ERNEST. That I am a poor devil.

D. JULIAN. The deuce! That's a famous discovery.

ERNEST. Nothing less.

D. JULIAN. But why are you so out of sorts with yourself? Is the play you talked of the other day not going on?

ERNEST. How can it? The going on is done by me going out of my wits.

D. JULIAN. How is this? Both the drama and inspiration are faithless to my poor friend.

ERNEST. This is how I stand. When I first conceived the idea, I imagined it full of promise, but when I attempt to give it form, and vest it in an appropriate stage garb, the result shows something extraordinary, difficult, undramatic and impossible.

D. JULIAN. How is it impossible? Come, tell me. You've excited my curiosity. [*Sits down on the sofa.*]

ERNEST. Imagine the principal personage, one who creates the drama and develops it, who gives it life and provokes the catastrophe, who, broadly, fills and possesses it, and yet who cannot make his way to the stage.

D. JULIAN. Is he so ugly, then? So repugnant or bad?

ERNEST. Not so. Bad as you or I may be—not worse. Neither good nor bad, and truly not repugnant. I am not such a cynic—neither a misanthrope, nor one so out of love with life as to fall into such unfairness.

D. JULIAN. What, then, is the reason?

ERNEST. The reason, Don Julian, is that there is no material room in the Scenario for this personage.

D. JULIAN. Holy Virgin! What do you mean? Is it by chance a mythological drama with Titans in it?

ERNEST. Titans, yes, but in the modern sense of the word.

D. JULIAN. That is to say——?

ERNEST. That is to say, this person is . . . *everybody*.

D. JULIAN. *Everybody!* You are right. There is no room for everybody on the stage. It is an incontrovertible truth that has more than once been demonstrated.

ERNEST. Then you agree with me?

D. JULIAN. Not entirely. Everybody may be condensed in a few types and characters. This is matter beyond my depth, but I have always understood that the masters have more than once accomplished it.

ERNEST. Yes, but in my case it is to condemn me, not to write my drama.

D. JULIAN. Why?

ERNEST. For many reasons it would be difficult to explain,—above all, at this late hour.

D. JULIAN. Never mind. Give me a few.

ERNEST. Look! Each individual of this entire mass, each head of this monster of a thousand heads, of this Titan of the century, whom I call *everybody*, takes part in my play for a flying moment, to utter but one word, fling a single glance. Perhaps his action in the tale consists of a smile, he appears but to vanish. Listless and absent-minded, he acts without passion, without anger, without guile, often for mere distraction's sake.

D. JULIAN. What then?

ERNEST. These light words, these fugitive glances, these indifferent smiles, all these evanescent sounds and this trivial evil, which may be called the insignificant rays of the dramatic light, condensed to one focus, to one group, result in conflagration or explosion, in strife and in victims. If I represent the whole by a few types or symbolical personages, I bestow upon each one that which is really dispersed among many, and such a result distorts my idea. I must bring types on the stage whose guile repels and is the less natural because evil in them has no object. This exposes me to a worse consequence, to the accusation of meaning to paint a cruel, corrupted, and debased society, when my sole pretention is to prove that not even the most insignificant actions are in themselves insignificant or lost for good or evil. For, concentrated by the mysterious influences of modern life, they may reach to immense effects.

D. JULIAN. Say no more, my friend. All this is metaphysics. A glimmer of light, perhaps, but through an infinitude of cloud. However, you understand these things better than I do. Letters of exchange, shares, stock, and discount, now—that's another matter.

ERNEST. No, no; you've common sense, and that's the chief thing.

D. JULIAN. You flatter me, Ernest.

ERNEST. But you follow me?

D. JULIAN. Not in the least. There ought to be a way out of the difficulty.

ERNEST. If that were all!

D. JULIAN. What! More?

ERNEST. Tell me what is the great dramatic spring?

D. JULIAN. My dear fellow, I don't exactly know what you mean by a dramatic spring. All I can tell you is that I have not the slightest interest in plays where love does not preponderate—above all unfortunate love, for I have enough of happy love at home.

ERNEST. Good, very good! Then in my play there can be little or no love.

D. JULIAN. So much the worse. Though I know nothing of your play, I suspect it will interest nobody.

ERNEST. So I have been telling you. Nevertheless, it is possible to put in a little love,—and jealousy too.

D. JULIAN. Ah, then, with an interesting intrigue skilfully developed, and some effective situations——

ERNEST. No, nothing of the sort. It will be all simple, ordinary, almost vulgar . . . so that the drama will not have any external action. The drama evolves within the personages: it advances slowly: to-day takes hold of a thought, to-morrow of a heart-beat, little by little, undermines the will.

D. JULIAN. But who understands all this? How are these interior ravages manifested? Who recounts them to the audience? In what way are they evident? Must we spend a whole evening hunting for a glance, a sigh, a gesture, a single word? My dear boy, this is not amusement. To cast us into such depths is to hurl us upon philosophy.

ERNEST. You but echo my own thought.

D. JULIAN. I have no wish to discourage you. You best know what you are about—there. Though the play seems rather colourless, heavy, uninteresting, perhaps if the *dénoûment* is sensational—and the explosion—eh?

ERNEST. Sensation! Explosion! Hardly, and that only just upon the fall of the curtain.

D. JULIAN. Which means that the play begins when the curtain falls?

ERNEST. I am inclined to admit it. But I will endeavour to give it a little warmth.

D. JULIAN. My dear lad, what you have to do is to write the *second* play, the one that begins where the first ends. For the other, according to your description, would be difficult to write, and is not worth the trouble.

ERNEST. 'Tis the conclusion I have come to myself.

D. JULIAN. Then we agree, thanks to your skill and logic. And what is the name?

ERNEST. That's another difficulty. I can find none.

D. JULIAN. What do you say? No name either?

ERNEST. No, unless, as Don Hermogenes[1] says, we could put it into Greek for greater clarity.

D. JULIAN. Of a surety, Ernest, you were dozing when I came in. You have been dreaming nonsense.

ERNEST. Dreaming! yes. Nonsense! perhaps. I talk both dreams and nonsense. But you are sensible and always right.

D. JULIAN. In this case it does not require much penetration. A drama in which the chief personage cannot appear; in which there is hardly any love; in which nothing happens but what happens every day; that begins with the fall of the curtain upon the last act, and which has no name. I don't know how it is to be written, still less how it is to be acted, how it is to find an audience, nor how it can be called a drama.

---

[1] A pedant in Moratin's *Comedia Nueva*, who quotes Greek incessantly to make himself better understood.—*Tran.*

ERNEST. Nevertheless, it is a drama, if I could only give it proper form, and that I can't do.

D. JULIAN. Do you wish to follow my advice?

ERNEST. Can you doubt it?—you, my friend, my benefactor, my second father! Don Julian!

D. JULIAN. Come, come, Ernest, don't let us drop into a sentimental drama on our own account instead of yours, which we have declared impossible. I asked you if you would take my advice.

ERNEST. And I said yes.

D. JULIAN. Then leave aside your plays. Go to bed, rest yourself, and come out shooting with me to-morrow. Kill a few partridges, and that will be an excuse for your not killing one or two characters, and not exposing yourself to the same fate at the hands of the public. After all, you may thank me for it.

ERNEST. I'll do no such thing. I mean to write that play.

D. JULIAN. But, my poor fellow, you've conceived it in mortal sin.

ERNEST. I don't know, but it is conceived. I feel it stir in my brain. It clamours for life, and I must give it to the world.

D. JULIAN. Can't you find another plot?

ERNEST. But this idea?

D. JULIAN. Send it to the devil.

ERNEST. Ah, Don Julian, you believe that an idea which has gripped the mind can be effaced and destroyed at our pleasure. I wanted to think out another play, but this accursed idea won't give it room, until it itself has seen the light.

D. JULIAN. God grant you a happy delivery.

ERNEST. That's the question, as Hamlet says.

D. JULIAN. Couldn't you cast it into the literary foundling hospital of anonymity?
[*In a low voice with an air of comical mystery.*]

ERNEST. Don Julian, I am a man of conscience. Good or bad, my children are legitimate. They bear my name.

D. JULIAN. [*Preparing to go.*] I have nothing more to say. What must be done will be done.

ERNEST. I wish it were so. Unfortunately, it is not done. But no matter; if I don't do it, somebody else will.

D. JULIAN. Then to work, and good luck, and may nobody rob you of your laurels.

SCENE III

Ernest, Don Julian, and Teodora.

TEODORA. [*Outside.*] Julian, Julian!

D. JULIAN. It's Teodora.

TEODORA. Are you there, Julian?

D. JULIAN. [*Going to the door.*] Yes, I'm here. Come in.

TEODORA. [*Entering.*] Good-evening, Ernest.

ERNEST. Good-evening, Teodora. Was the singing good?

TEODORA. As usual; and have you been working much?

ERNEST. As usual; nothing.

TEODORA. Then you'd have done better to come with us. They all asked after you.

ERNEST. It seems that everybody is interested in me.

D. JULIAN. I should think so, since *everybody* is to be the principal personage of your play. You may imagine if they are anxious to be on good terms with you.

TEODORA. A play?

D. JULIAN. Hush! 'Tis a mystery. Ask no questions. Neither title, nor characters, nor action, nor catastrophe —the sublime! Good-night, Ernest. Come, Teodora.

ERNEST. Adieu, Don Julian.

TEODORA. Till to-morrow.

ERNEST. Good-night.

TEODORA. [*To Don Julian.*] How preoccupied Mercedes was!

D. JULIAN. And Severo was in a rage.

TEODORA. Why, I wonder.

D. JULIAN. How do I know? On the other hand, Pepito chattered enough for both.

TEODORA. He always does, and nobody escapes his tongue.

D. JULIAN. He's a character for Ernest's play.
[*Exeunt Teodora, and Don Julian by right.*]

SCENE IV

ERNEST. Let Don Julian say what he will, I won't abandon the undertaking. That would be signal cowardice. Never retreat—always forward. [*Rises and begins to walk about in an agitated way. Then approaches the balcony.*] Protect me, night. In thy blackness, rather than in the azure clearness of day, are outlined the luminous shapes of inspiration. Lift your roofs, you thousand houses of this great town, as well for a poet in dire necessity as for the devil on two sticks

who so wantonly exposed you. Let me see the men
and women enter your drawing-rooms and boudoirs in
search of the night's rest after fevered pleasures abroad.
Let my acute hearing catch the stray words of all those
who inquired for me of Don Julian and Teodora. As
the scattered rays of light, when gathered to a focus by
diaphanous crystal, strike flame, and darkness is forged
by the crossed bars of shadow; as mountains are made
from grains of earth, and seas from drops of water: so
will I use your wasted words, your vague smiles, your
eager glances, and build my play of all those thousand
trivialities dispersed in *cafés*, at reunions, theatres, and
spectacles, and that float now in the air. Let the
modest crystal of my intelligence be the lens which
will concentrate light and shadow, from which will
spring the dramatic conflagration and the tragic explosion
of the catastrophe. Already my play takes shape. It
has even a title now, for there, under the lamp-shade,
I see the immortal work of the immortal Florentine.
It offers me in Italian what in good Spanish it would
be risky and futile audacity either to write on paper
or pronounce on the stage. Francesca and Paolo,
assist me with the story of your loves! [*Sits down
and prepares to write.*] The play . . . the play
begins. . . . First page—there, 'tis no longer white. It
has a name. [*Writing.*] *The Great Galeoto.* [*Writes
feverishly.*]

END OF PROLOGUE

ACT I

SCENE—*A drawing-room in Don Julian's house. At the back of stage a large door, and beyond a passage separating it from the dining-room door, which remains closed throughout the act. On the left a balcony, and beyond it a door. On the right two doors. On the stage a table, an arm-chair, handsome and luxurious mounting. Hour, towards sunset.*

SCENE I

Teodora and Don Julian. Teodora near the balcony; Don Julian seated on the sofa, lost in thought.

TEODORA. What a lovely sunset! what clouds and light, and what a sky! Suppose it were true, as the poets say, and our fathers believed, that our fate is stamped upon the azure heaven! Were the mysterious secret of human destiny traced by the stars upon the sapphire sphere, and this splendid evening should hold the cipher of ours, what happiness it must disclose! what a smiling future! What a life in our life, and what radiance in our heaven! Is it not so, Julian? [*She approaches Don Julian.*] Ah, plunged in thought, I see! Come and look out. What, no word for me?

D. JULIAN. [*Absently.*] What is it?

TEODORA. [*Coming near.*] You have not been listening to me!

D. JULIAN. You have my heart ever—who are its magnet and its centre. But my mind is apt to be besieged by preoccupations, cares, business——

TEODORA. They are the plague of my life, since they rob me, if not of my husband's affections, at least of some of his attention. But what is the matter, Julian? [*Affectionately.*] Something worries you. Is it serious, that you are so solemn and so silent? If it should be trouble, Julian, remember that I have a right to share it. My joys are yours, and your sorrows are no less mine.

D. JULIAN. Sorrows! Troubles! Are you not happy? Do I not possess in you the living embodiment of joy? With those cheeks so ruddy in the glow of health, and those dear eyes, clear like your soul and resplendent as the sky, and I the owner of all you, could pain, or shadow, or grief teach me I am other than the happiest man alive?

TEODORA. It is a business annoyance, perhaps?

D. JULIAN. Money never yet forced sleep or appetite to forsake me. I have never felt aversion, much less contempt for it, so it follows that the article has flowed easily into my coffers. I was rich, I am rich; and until Don Julian of Garagarga dies of old age, please God and his own good fortune, he will remain, if not the wealthiest, certainly the surest, banker of Madrid, Cadiz, and Oporto.

TEODORA. Then what is your preoccupation?

D. JULIAN. I was thinking—'tis a good thought, too.

TEODORA. Naturally, since 'tis yours.

D. JULIAN. Flatterer! you would spoil me.

TEODORA. But I am still unenlightened.

D. JULIAN. There is an important matter I want to achieve.

TEODORA. Connected with the new works?

D. JULIAN. No; it has nothing to do with stone or iron.

TEODORA. What, then?

D. JULIAN. It is a question of kindness—a sacred debt of old date.

TEODORA. [*Gleefully.*] Oh, I can guess now.

D. JULIAN. So!

TEODORA. You mean Ernest.

D. JULIAN. You are right.

TEODORA. Yes, yes, you must. Poor lad! he's so good and noble and generous.

D. JULIAN. Quite his father's son—the model of a loyal hidalgo.

TEODORA. And then so clever! Only twenty-six, and a prodigy! what doesn't he know?

D. JULIAN. Know! I should think he *did* know. That's nothing—rather, that's the worst of it. While he is wandering in the sphere of sublime thought, I fear he's not likely to learn much of a world so deceptive and prosaic as ours, which takes no interest in the subtleties of the mind until three centuries after genius has been buried.

TEODORA. But with you for a guide, Julian—you don't intend to abandon him yet a while, surely?

D. JULIAN. God forbid. I should be black-hearted indeed if I would so readily forget all I owe his father. Don Juan of Acedo risked for my family name and wealth, ay, almost his life. Should this lad need mine, he might ask it, and welcome. 'Twould be but just payment of the debt my name represents.

TEODORA. Well said, Julian. It is like you.

D. JULIAN. You remember, about a year ago, I heard my good friend was dead, and his son was left badly off. I lost no time, caught the train to Gerona, nearly used force, and carried the boy back here. When he stood in the middle of this room I said to him: 'You are master here; you may command me and mine. Since I owe your father everything, you must regard me in the light of his representative. If I fall short, my desire is to come as near as possible to him. As for the amount of affection I have to dispose of—we'll see if I don't out-race him there.'

TEODORA. I remember it well. The soft-hearted fellow burst out crying, and clung to you like a child.

D. JULIAN. He's but a child, as you say. That's why we must think and plan for him. And 'twas of that I was so seriously thinking a moment ago. I was meditating a half-formed project, while you, dear, wanted me to contemplate a panorama of radiant cloud and scarlet sun that cannot compare with the sun that shines in my own heaven.

TEODORA. I cannot divine your idea. What is it you project doing for Ernest?

D. JULIAN. Those are my words.

TEODORA. But is there something yet undone that you expect to discover? He has lived with us for the past year like one of ourselves. Were he your son, or a brother of mine, could you show him more tenderness, I more affection?

D. JULIAN. It is much, but not enough.

TEODORA. Not enough! I fancy,——

D. JULIAN. You are thinking of the present, and I of the future.

TEODORA. Oh! the future! That is easily settled. See, he lives here with us as long as he likes, for years. It is his home. Then when the just and natural law prompts him to fall in love and desire another, we will marry him. You will nobly share your wealth with him, and we will lead them from the altar to their own house,—*he* and *she*! The proverb, you know, says wisely, 'for each wedded pair a house.' He will live just a little away from us, but that will be no reason for our forgetting him, or loving him less. I see it all distinctly. They are happy, and we even happier. They have children, of course, and we perhaps more—well, at least, one little girl, who will fall in love with Ernest's son, and to whom we will marry her by and by.

[*Spoken playfully, with volubility, grace, blushes, and lively gesture, according to the actress's talents.*]

D. JULIAN. But where in heaven's name are you going to stop? [*Laughing.*]

TEODORA. You spoke of his future, Julian, and I've sketched it. If not this one, I will neither approve nor accept it.

D. JULIAN. How like you, Teodora! but——

TEODORA. Ah, there is a but already.

D. JULIAN. Listen, Teodora. It is but a debt we owe to look after the poor fellow as if he were a relative, and obligation runs with the exactions of our affection. So much for himself, so much for his father's son. But every human action is complex, has two points of view, and every medal has its reverse. Which means, Teodora, that you must understand it is a very different matter to give and receive favours; and that in the end Ernest might feel my protection a humiliation. He's a high-spirited, fine lad, a trifle haughty perhaps, and it is imperative there should be an end to his present position. We may, if we can, do more for him, but we must seem to do less.

TEODORA. How so?

D. JULIAN. We'll see—but here he comes—— [*Looks down the stage.*]

TEODORA. Hush!

SCENE II

Don Julian, Teodora, and Ernest behind.

D. JULIAN. Welcome!

ERNEST. Don Julian!—and Teodora! [*Salutes absently. Sits down near the table in pensive silence.*]

DON JULIAN. [*Approaching him.*] What's the matter?

ERNEST. Nothing.

D. JULIAN. You look as if something ailed you—your preoccupation reveals it. No trouble, I hope?

ERNEST. Nonsense.

D. JULIAN. Nor disappointment?

ERNEST. None whatever.

D. JULIAN. I don't annoy you?

ERNEST. You! good heavens! [*Rises and comes toward him effusively.*] You speak out of the right of friendship and affection, and you read me through and through. Yes, sir; there is indeed something the matter. I will tell you, if you, and you also, Teodora, out of your pity, will hold me excused. I am an ungrateful fool, a mere boy, in truth, deserving neither of your kindness nor of your affection. Possessing such a father and such a sister, I ought to be happy, with no care for the morrow. But it is not so. I blush to explain it,—can't you understand?—Yes, yes, you must see how false my position is. I live here on alms. [*With energy.*]

TEODORA. Such a word——

ERNEST. Teodora!

TEODORA. Affronts us.

ERNEST. I expressed myself ill—but it is so.

D. JULIAN. I say it is not so. If any one in this house lives upon alms, and those no slight ones, it is I and not you.

ERNEST. I am acquainted, sir, with the story of two loyal friends, and of some money matters long forgotten. It does honour to my father and to his hidalgic race. But I am shamed in profiting by it. I am young, Don Julian, and although I may not be worth much, there ought still to be some way for me to earn my bread. It may be pride or folly, I cannot say. But I remember what my father used to say: 'What you can do yourself, never ask another to do. What you can earn, never owe to any one else.'

D. JULIAN. So that my services humiliate and degrade you. You count your friends importunate creditors.

TEODORA. Reason may be on your side, Ernest, and in knowledge you are not deficient, but, believe me, in this case the heart alone speaks with wisdom.

D. JULIAN. Your father did not find me so ungenerous or so proud.

TEODORA. Ah, friendship was then a very different thing.

ERNEST. Teodora!

TEODORA. [*To Don Julian.*] What a noble anxiety he displays!

ERNEST. I know I seem ungrateful—I feel it—and an idiot to boot. Forgive me, Don Julian.

D. JULIAN. His head is a forge.

TEODORA. [*Also apart to Don Julian.*] He doesn't live in this world.

D. JULIAN. Just so. He's full of depth and learning, and lets himself be drowned in a pool of water.

ERNEST. [*Meditatively.*] True, I know little of life, and am not well fitted to make my way through it. But I divine it, and shudder, I know not why. Shall I founder on the world's pool as upon the high sea? I may not deny that it terrifies me far more than the deep ocean. The sea only reaches the limit set by the loose sand: over all space travel the emanations of the pool. A strong man's arms can struggle with the waves of the sea, but no one can struggle against subtle miasma. But if I fall, I must not feel the humiliation of defeat. I wish and pray that at the last moment I may see the approach of the sea that will bear me away at its will; see the sword that is to pierce me, the rock against which I am to be crushed. I must measure my adversary's strength, and despise it falling, despise it dying, instead of tamely breathing the venom scattered through the ambient air.

D. JULIAN. [*To Teodora.*] Didn't I tell you he was going out of his mind?

TEODORA. But, Ernest, where are you wandering?

D. JULIAN. Yes. What has all this to do with the matter?

ERNEST. Sir, I have come to the conclusion that others, seeing me housed and fed here, are saying of me what I long have thought. They see me constantly driving out with you, in the morning walking with Teodora or Mercedes, in your opera-box, hunting on your lands, and daily occupying the same place at your table. Though you would like to think otherwise, in one way or another the gossip runs: Who is he? Is he a relation? Not so. The secretary? Still less. A partner? If a partner, it may be accepted he brings little or nothing to the general fund. So they chatter.

D. JULIAN. By no means. You are raving.

ERNEST. I beg to contradict you.

D. JULIAN. Then give me a name.

ERNEST. Sir——

D. JULIAN. One will do.

ERNEST. There is one at hand—upstairs.

D. JULIAN. Name him.

ERNEST. Don Severo.

D. JULIAN. My brother?

ERNEST. Exactly, your brother? Will that suffice? or shall we add his respected wife, Doña Mercedes? and Pepito, their son? What have you to say then?

D. JULIAN. That Severo is a fool, Mercedes an idle chatterer, and the lad a puppy.

ERNEST. They only repeat what they hear.

D. JULIAN. It is not true. This is false reasoning. Between gentlemen, when the intention is honourable, what can the opinion of the world really matter? The meaner it is, the loftier our disdain of it.

ERNEST. 'Tis nobly said, and is what all well-bred men feel. But I have been taught that gossip, whether inspired by malice or not, which is according to each one's natural tendency, begins in a lie and generally ends in truth. Does gossip, as it grows, disclose the hidden sin? Is it a reflex of the past, or does it invent evil and give it existence? Does it set its accursed seal upon an existent fault, or merely breed that which was yet not, and furnish the occasion for wrong? Should we call the slanderer infamous or severe? the accomplice or the divulger? the public avenger or the tempter? Does he arrest or precipitate our fall? wound through taste or duty? and when he condemns, is it from justice or from spite? Perhaps both, Don Julian. Who can say? though time, occasion, and facts may show.

D. JULIAN. See here, Ernest, I don't understand an iota of all this philosophising. I presume 'tis on such nonsense you waste your intelligence. But I don't want you to be vexed or worried. It's true—you really wish for austere independence, to stand alone at a post of honour?

ERNEST. Don Julian!

D. JULIAN. Answer me.

ERNEST. [*Joyously*]. Yes.

D. JULIAN. Then count it gained. At this very moment I have no secretary. I am expecting one from London. But nobody would suit me better than a certain young fool, who is enamoured of poverty. [*Speaks in pleasant reproach.*] His work and salary will, of course, be settled as any one else's, though he be a son to one who cherishes him as such.

ERNEST. Don Julian!

D. JULIAN. [*Affecting comical severity.*] Remember, I am an exacting business man, and I have not the habit of giving my money away for nothing. I intend to get as much as possible out of you, and work you hard. In my house the bread of just labour alone is consumed. By the clock, ten hours, starting at daybreak, and when I choose to be severe, you will see that Severo himself is no match for me. So, before the world you pose as the victim of my selfishness ... but in private, dear boy, ever the same, the centre of my dearest affections. [*Unable to maintain former tone, Don Julian breaks off, and holds his hand out to Ernest.*]

ERNEST. [*Deeply moved.*] Don Julian!

D. JULIAN. You accept, then?

ERNEST. I am yours to command.

TEODORA. [*To Don Julian.*] At last you have tamed the savage.

ERNEST. [*To Don Julian.*] Anything for your sake.

D. JULIAN. So would I have you always, Ernest. And now I have to write to my London correspondent, and thank him, and while recognising the extraordinary merit of his Englishman, whom he extols to the skies, regret that I have already engaged a young man. [*Walks toward the first door on the right hand.*] This is how we stand for the present; but in the future—it will be as partners. [*Returns with an air of mystery.*]

TEODORA. Stop, Julian, I beg of you. Can't you see that he will take alarm? [*Don Julian goes out on the right, and laughs to himself, looking back at Ernest.*]

SCENE III

Teodora and Ernest. Towards the end of the last scene twilight has fallen, so that at this moment the room is in deep shadow.

ERNEST. I am dazed by so much kindness. How can I ever repay it? [*He sits down on the sofa, displaying great emotion. Teodora walks over and stands beside him*].

TEODORA. By ejecting the spirit of pride and distrust; by being sensible and believing that we truly love you, that we will never change; and by putting full faith in all Julian's promises. His word is sacred, Ernest, and in him you will always have a father, in me a sister.

SCENE IV

Teodora, Ernest, Doña Mercedes, and Don Severo. The latter remain standing behind as they enter. The room is quite dark, save for a glimmer of light shed from the balcony, whither Ernest and Teodora have moved.

ERNEST. How good you are!

TEODORA. And you, what a boy! After to-day I hope you have done with sadness—eh?

ERNEST. Quite.

MERCEDES. [*Outside, speaking low.*] How dark it is!

SEVERO. [*In same tone.*] Come away, Mercedes.

MERCEDES. [*Crossing the threshold.*] There is nobody here.

SEVERO. [*Detaining her.*] Yes, there is. [*Both stand a while peering.*]

ERNEST. Teodora, my whole life, a thousand lives would still not be enough to offer you in return for your kindness. Don't judge me by my morose temper. I cannot lend a showy front to my affections, but, believe me, I do know how to love—and hate as well. My heart can beat to bursting under the lash of either sentiment.

MERCEDES. [*To Severo.*] What are they saying?

SEVERO. Something odd, but I hear imperfectly. [*Teodora and Ernest go out on the balcony, speaking low.*]

MERCEDES. 'Tis Ernest.

SEVERO. And she—I suppose—is——

MERCEDES. Teodora.

SEVERO. Their eternal tricks—always together. I can stand no more of this. And their words? I mustn't put it off any longer——

MERCEDES. True, Severo. Come away. It is certainly your duty, since everybody is talking.

SEVERO. Yes, I must open Julian's eyes—to-day, at once.

MERCEDES. The fellow has impudence enough, and to spare.

SEVERO. By all that's holy—so has she.

MERCEDES. Poor girl! She's but a child. Leave her to me.

TEODORA. Another house? Surely no. You wouldn't leave us? What an idea! Julian would never consent.

SEVERO. [*To Doña Mercedes.*] I should think not indeed, neither would I. [*Aloud.*] Ah, Teodora, you didn't see me? This is how you receive your guests.

TEODORA. [*Coming from the balcony.*] Don Severo! I am delighted.

MERCEDES. Is there no dinner this evening? It's near the hour.

TEODORA. Mercedes too!

MERCEDES. Yes, Teodora.

SEVERO. [*Aside.*] She is a capital actress. What a creature!

TEODORA. I must ring for lights. [*Touches the bell on the table.*]

SEVERO. Quite so. Every one likes plenty of light.

SERVANT. Madam?

TEODORA. Bring the lamps, Genaro. [*Exit servant.*]

SEVERO. He who follows the narrow path of loyalty and duty, and is always that which he appears to be, need never fear the light, nor blush in its glare.
[*The servant enters with lamps, the stage is brilliantly illuminated. After a pause.*]

TEODORA. [*Laughing naturally.*] So I should think, and such, I imagine, is the general opinion. [*Looks at Mercedes.*]

MERCEDES. I suppose so.

SEVERO. Hulloa, Don Ernest! what were you doing out there? Were you with Teodora when we came in! [*Speaks with marked intention.*]

ERNEST. [*Coldly.*] I was here as you see.

SEVERO. The deuce you were! It is rather dark to see. [*Approaches him with outstretched hand, looking fixedly at him. Teodora and Mercedes converse apart. Aside.*] His face is flushed, and he appears to have been crying. In this world only children and lovers weep. [*Aloud.*] And Julian?

TEODORA. He went away to write a letter.

ERNEST. [*Aside.*] Though I have patience to spare, this man tries me hard.

SEVERO. [*To Teodora.*] I am going to see him. There is still time before dinner?

TEODORA. Plenty.

SEVERO. Good. Then to work. [*Aside, rubbing his hands, and looking back at Ernest and Teodora. Aloud.*] Good-bye.

TEODORA. Goodbye.

SEVERO. [*Rancorously, from the door.*] My faith!

SCENE V

Teodora, Doña Mercedes, and Ernest. The ladies occupy the sofa, and Ernest stands near them.

MERCEDES. [*To Ernest.*] We did not see you to-day.

ERNEST. No, madam.

MERCEDES. Nor Pepito?

ERNEST. No.

MERCEDES. He is upstairs alone.

ERNEST. [*Aside.*] Let him stop there.

MERCEDES. [*Gravely and mysteriously to Teodora.*] I wish he would go. I want to speak to you.

TEODORA. Indeed?

MERCEDES. [*In same tone.*] Yes, it is something very serious.

TEODORA. Well, begin!

MERCEDES. Why doesn't he go?

TEODORA. [*In a low voice.*] I don't understand you.

MERCEDES. Courage! [*Takes her hand and clasps it affectionately. Teodora looks at her in sombre question.*] Send him about his business.

TEODORA. If you insist. Ernest, will you do me a favour?

ERNEST. Gladly—with a thousand wills.

MERCEDES. [*Aside.*] One were still too many.

TEODORA. Then go upstairs—to Pepito——But it might bore you to carry a message.

ERNEST. By no means.

MERCEDES. [*Aside.*] In what a sweet, soft voice he speaks to her!

TEODORA. Tell him—ask him if he has renewed our subscription at the Opera as I told him. He knows about it.

ERNEST. With pleasure—this very moment.

TEODORA. Thanks, Ernest, I am sorry——

ERNEST. Nonsense. [*Exit.*]

TEODORA. Adieu!

SCENE VI

Teodora and Doña Mercedes.

TEODORA. Something serious? You alarm me, Mercedes. Such mystery! What can it mean?

MERCEDES. It is indeed very serious.

TEODORA. Concerning whom?

MERCEDES. All of you.

TEODORA. All of us?

MERCEDES. Julian, Ernest, and you.

TEODORA. All three?

MERCEDES. Yes, all three. [*Short pause. Both women stare at each other.*]

TEODORA. Then make haste.

MERCEDES. [*Aside.*] I should like to——but, no; I must go gently in this unsavoury affair. [*Aloud.*] Listen, Teodora. My husband is, after all, your husband's brother, and in life and death our fortunes are one. So that we owe one another in all things protection, help, and advice,—is it not so? To-day it may be I who offer assistance, and to-morrow, should I need it, I unblushingly claim it of you.

TEODORA. You may count upon it, Mercedes. But come to the end of the matter now.

MERCEDES. Up to to-day, Teodora, I shrank from this step, but Severo urges me. 'It can't go on,' he insists. 'My brother's honour and my own self-esteem forbid me to witness that which fills me with shame and sorrow. On all sides am I assailed with innuendoes, with the smiles, the covert glances and the reproaches of my friends. There must be an end to this low gossip about us.'

TEODORA. Continue, pray.

MERCEDES. Then heed me. [*They exchange a prolonged gaze.*]

TEODORA. Tell me, what is the gossip?

MERCEDES. The murmuring of the river tells us that its waters are swollen.

TEODORA. I understand nothing of your river and its swollen waters, but do not drive me wild.

MERCEDES. [*Aside.*] Poor child! My heart grieves for her. [*Aloud.*] So you do not understand me?

TEODORA. I? not in the least.

MERCEDES. [*Aside.*] How stupid she is! [*Aloud, energetically.*] You make a laughing-stock of him.

TEODORA. Of whom?

MERCEDES. Why, of your husband, of course.

TEODORA. [*Impetuously, rising.*] Julian! what a falsehood! What wretch could say so? Julian would strike him!

MERCEDES. [*Endeavouring to soothe her and make her sit down.*] He would need a good many hands, then; for, if report speak truly, he would have to strike the entire town.

TEODORA. But what does it all mean? What is the mystery, and what is this talk of the town?

MERCEDES. So you're sorry?

TEODORA. I am sorry. But what is it?

MERCEDES. You see, Teodora, you are quite a child. At your age one is so often thoughtless and light, and then such bitter tears are afterwards shed. You still don't understand me?

TEODORA. No, what has such a case to do with me?

MERCEDES. It is the story of a scoundrel and the story of a lady——

TEODORA. [*Eagerly.*] Whose name——?

MERCEDES. Her name——

TEODORA. Oh, what does it matter?
 [*Teodora moves away from Mercedes, who shifts her seat on the sofa to follow her. The double movement of repugnance and aloofness on Teodora's part, and of insistence and protection on Mercedes', is very marked.*]

MERCEDES. The man is a shabby-hearted betrayer, who, for one hour of pleasure, would thrust upon the woman a life of sorrow: the husband's dishonour, the ruin of a family, and she left shamed and condemned to social penitence in the world's disdain, and to keener punishment still at the whip of her own conscience.
 [*Here Teodora, avoiding Mercedes, reaches the edge of the sofa, bows her head and covers her face with both hands. At last she understands.*]

MERCEDES. [*Aside.*] Poor little thing! She touches me. [*Aloud.*] This man is not worthy of you, Teodora.

TEODORA. But, madam, what is the drift of all this blind emotion? Do not imagine that my eyes are dimmed with fear or horror or tears. They burn with the flame of anger. To whom can such words be addressed? What man do you mean? Is it, perchance——?

MERCEDES. Ernest.

TEODORA. Ah! [*Pause.*] And the woman I? Not so? [*Mercedes nods and Teodora rises again.*] Then listen to me, though I may offend you. I know not who is the viler, the inventor of this tale or you who repeat it. Shame upon the meanness that formed the idea, and shame upon the villainy that spreads it! It is so abominable, so fatal, that I almost feel myself criminal because I cannot instantly reject the thought and forget it. Heavens! could I suppose or credit such baseness? Because of his misfortunes I loved him. He was like a brother to me, and Julian was his providence. And he so noble and thorough a gentleman! [*Stands staring at Mercedes, then turns away her face. Aside.*] How she inspects me! I scarcely like to say a good word for him to her. My God! I am compelled already to act a part.

MERCEDES. Be calm, child.

TEODORA. [*Raising her voice.*] Oh, what anguish! I feel cold and inconsolable. Stained in this way by public opinion! Oh, my dearest mother, and you, Julian, my heart's beloved. [*She falls sobbing into a chair on the left, and Mercedes strives to console her.*]

MERCEDES. I did not imagine—forgive me—don't cry. There, I didn't really believe it was serious. I knew your past exonerated you. But as the case stands, you must admit that out of every hundred a hundred would accuse you and Julian of excessive rashness, or say you had led the world to conclude the worst. You a girl of twenty, Julian a man of forty, and Ernest between you, with his head full of romantic thoughts. On the one hand, a husband given up to business, on the other a youth to dreams, every day bringing its opportunity, and you there, unoccupied, in the flush of romance. It was wrong for people to conclude the worst because they saw you walking with him, and saw him so often at the theatre with you. But, Teodora, in reason and justice

I think that, if the world was bent on seeing evil, you furnished the occasion. Permit me to point out to you that the fault which society most fiercely chastises, pursues most relentlessly and cruelly, and in every varied imaginable way, both in man and woman is—don't frown so, Teodora—is *temerity*.

TEODORA. [*Turning to Mercedes without having heard her.*] And you say that Julian——

MERCEDES. Is the laughing-stock of the town, and you——

TEODORA. Oh, I! That's no matter. But Julian!—Oh, oh, so good, so chivalrous! If he only knew——

MERCEDES. He will know, for at this very moment Severo is telling him.

TEODORA. What!

JULIAN. [*Inside.*] That will do.

TEODORA. Oh, goodness!

JULIAN. Let me alone.

TEODORA. Come away, quickly.

MERCEDES. [*Rushing with Teodora towards first door on the right.*] Yes, yes, quickly. What folly! [*Teodora and Mercedes go to the right.*]

TEODORA. [*Stopping suddenly.*] But wherefore, since I am not guilty? Not only does miserable calumny stain us, but it degrades us. It is so steeped in evil, that, against all evidence, its very breath takes the bloom off our consciences. Why should an idle terror cast its mean influence over me? [*At this moment Don Julian appears on the threshold of the first door on the right hand side, and behind him stands Don Severo.*]

TEODORA. Julian!

D. JULIAN. Teodora! [*She runs over to him, and he folds her in a passionate embrace.*] Here in my arms, dearest. It is the home of your honour.

SCENE VII

Teodora, Doña Mercedes, Don Julian, and Don Severo. Don Julian and Doña Mercedes form the centre group.

D. JULIAN. Let it pass for this once, but, please God! there's an end of it. Whoever in future shall stain this face with tears [*pointing to Teodora*], I swear, and mean it, will never again cross the threshold of my house—though he should be my own brother. [*Pause. Don Julian soothes and comforts Teodora.*]

D. SEVERO. I only mentioned common report.

D. JULIAN. Infamous!

D. SEVERO. It may be so.

D. JULIAN. It is.

D. SEVERO. Well, let me tell you what every one says.

D. JULIAN. Filth! abominable lies.

D. SEVERO. Then repeating them——

D. JULIAN. 'Tis not the way to put an end to them.

[*Pause.*]

D. SEVERO. You are wrong.

D. JULIAN. Right—more than right. A fine thing it would be if I let you carry the mire of the street into my drawing-room!

D. SEVERO. But I will do so.

D. JULIAN. You shall not.

D. SEVERO. You bear my name.

D. JULIAN. Enough.

D. SEVERO. And your honour——

D. JULIAN. Remember that you are in my wife's presence. [*Pause.*]

D. SEVERO. [*In a low voice to Don Julian.*] If our father saw you——

D. JULIAN. What do you mean, Severo?

MERCEDES. Hush! Here is Ernest.

TEODORA. [*Aside.*] How dreadful! If he should know—— [*Teodora turns away her face, and holds her head bent. Don Julian looks at her questioningly.*]

SCENE VIII

Teodora, Doña Mercedes, Don Julian, Don Severo, Ernest and Pepito grouped from left to right. On entering, Pepito stands on Don Julian's side and Ernest walks over to Teodora.

ERNEST. [*Looking at Don Julian and Teodora. Aside.*] He and she! It is no illusion. Can it be what I feared? what that fool told me. [*Referring to Pepito, who at that moment enters behind.*] It was not his invention.

PEPITO. [*Staring strangely about.*] My salutations to all, and good appetite—as it is dinner-time. Here are the tickets, Teodora. Don Julian——

TEODORA. Thanks, Pepito. [*Accepts them mechanically.*]

ERNEST. [*To Don Julian in a low voice.*] What's the matter with Teodora?

D. JULIAN. Nothing.

ERNEST. [*In same tone.*] She is pale, and has been crying.

D. JULIAN. [*Angrily.*] Don't busy yourself about my wife. [*Pause. Don Julian and Ernest exchange glances.*]

ERNEST. [*Aside.*] The wretches! They've completed their work.

PEPITO. [*In a low voice to his mother, pointing to Ernest.*] He ought to have a strait-jacket. I quizzed him about Teodora. Poof! 'Pon my word, I thought he'd kill me.

ERNEST. [*Aloud, with resolution and sadness.*] Don Julian, I have thought over your generous offer, and much as I've already abused your kindness, it goes sorely against me to refuse it now. But, sir, I feel that I ought to reject this post you offer me.

D. JULIAN. Why?

ERNEST. Because I am so fashioned,—a poet and a dreamer. My father, sir, trained me for no career. I want to travel; I am restless and liable to revolt. I am not capable of settling down like another. Like a new Columbus, I am bitten by the spirit of adventure. But we will appeal to Don Severo. He will decide if I am right.

D. SEVERO. You speak like the book of wisdom and like a man of sense. I have been thinking as you do for a long while.

D. JULIAN. Since when have you felt this itch for new worlds and travel? When did you make up your mind to leave us? And the means?—where are they?

D. SEVERO. He wants to go away—to some place more to his taste than here. To be just, Julian, the rest is your affair. Give him as much as he wants, too, for this is no time for economy.

ERNEST. [*To Don Severo.*] I don't traffic with dishonour, nor receive alms. [*Pause.*] Well, it must be so; and as our parting would be a sad one—for in this life, who knows? I may never come back, and may not see them again—it is better that we should shake hands now, here, Don Julian, and have it over. Thus we snap the tie, and you forgive my selfishness. [*Deeply moved.*]

D. SEVERO. [*Aside.*] How they stare at one another!

TEODORA. [*Aside.*] What a noble fellow!

ERNEST. [*To Don Julian.*] Why do you withhold your hand? It is our last adieu, Don Julian. [*Goes toward him with outstretched hands. Don Julian embraces him.*]

D. JULIAN. No, lad. The question well considered, this is neither the first nor the last. It is the cordial embrace of two honourable men. You must not mention your mad project again.

D. SEVERO. Then he is not going away?

D. JULIAN. Never. I have not the habit of changing my mind or the plans I have matured because of a boy's caprice or a madman's folly. And I have still less intention of weakly subjecting my actions to the town's idle gossip.

D. SEVERO. Julian!

D. JULIAN. Enough. Dinner is served.

ERNEST. Father, I cannot——

D. JULIAN. But what if I believe you can? Or does my authority begin to bore you?

ERNEST. I beg you——

D. JULIAN. Come, dinner is ready. Give your arm to Teodora, and take her in.

ERNEST. [*Looking at her, but holding back.*] To Teodora!

TEODORA. [*With a similar emotion.*] Ernest!

D. JULIAN. Yes, as usual.
   [*There is a movement of uncertainty on both sides; finally Ernest approaches and Teodora takes his arm, but neither dares to look at the other, and both are abrupt and violently agitated.*]

D. JULIAN. [*To Pepito.*] And you! The deuce, why don't you offer your arm to your mother? My good brother Severo will take mine. So, quite a family party, and now let pleasure flow with the wine in our glasses. So there are gossips about? Well, let them chatter and scream. A farthing for all they can say. I shouldn't object to a glass house, that they might have the pleasure of staring in at Teodora and Ernest together, and learn how little I care for their spite and their calumnies. Each man to his fancy.

[*Enter servant in black suit and white tie.*]

SERVANT. Dinner is served.

[*The dining-room door opens and displays a well-appointed table.*]

D. JULIAN. Let us look after our life, since it will be the affair of others to look after our death. Come. [*Invites the others to pass.*]

TEODORA. Mercedes.

MERCEDES. Teodora.

TEODORA. I pray you, Mercedes.

[*Doña Mercedes passes in with Pepito and takes her place at the table. Ernest and Teodora stand plunged in thought, Ernest looking anxiously at her.*]

D. JULIAN. [*Aside.*] He is looking at her, and there are tears in her eyes. [*Teodora, walking unsteadily and struggling with emotion, slowly follows the others inside.*]

D. JULIAN. [*To Severo.*] Are they talking together?

D. SEVERO. I don't know, but I think it very probable.

D. JULIAN. Why are they looking back at us? Both! Did you notice? I wonder why.

D. SEVERO. You see, you are growing reasonable at last!

D. JULIAN. No, I've caught your madness. Ah, how sure a thing is calumny! It pierces straight to the heart.

ACT II

Scene represents a small room almost poorly furnished. Door at the end, on the right another door, and on the left a balcony. A book-case, a table, an arm-chair. On the table Don Julian's portrait in a frame, beside it an empty frame; both small and alike. On the table an unlighted lamp, the 'Divina Commedia,' open at the Francesca episode, and close to it a morsel of burnt paper. Papers scattered about, and the MS. of a play. A few chairs. Time, day.

SCENE I

Enter Don Julian. Don Severo and servant below.

D. SEVERO. Don Ernest is out?

SERVANT. Yes, sir. He went out early.

D. SEVERO. No matter. We'll wait. I suppose he will be in sooner or later.

SERVANT. I should think so. Nobody could be more punctual than he.

D. SEVERO. That will do.

SERVANT. Certainly, sir. If you want anything, you'll find me downstairs. [*Exit servant.*]

SCENE II

Don Julian and Don Severo.

D. SEVERO. [*Looking round.*] How modest!

D. JULIAN. Poor is a better word.

D. SEVERO. What a lodging! [*Opens the door and peeps in.*] An alcove, this study, and an outer room—and that's all.

D. JULIAN. And thereby hangs the devil's own tale of human ingratitude, of bastard sentiment, of miserable passions, and of blackguard calumny. And whether you tell it quickly or at length, there's never an end to it.

D. SEVERO. It is the work of chance.

D. JULIAN. Not so, my dear fellow. It was the work of—well, I know whom.

D. SEVERO. Meaning me?

D. JULIAN. Yes, you as well. And before you the empty-pated idlers whom it behoved to busy themselves shamelessly about my honour and my wife's. And I, coward, mean, and jealous, I let the poor fellow go, despite my evidence of his upright nature. I responded to his nobler conduct by black ingratitude. Yes, ingratitude. You see my ostentatious wealth, the luxury of my surroundings and equipages, and the credit of my firm. Well, do you know where all that comes from?

D. SEVERO. I have quite forgotten.

D. JULIAN. Justly said,—forgotten! Such is the natural reward of every generous action, of every unusual impulse that prompts one man to help another quietly, without a flourish of trumpet or self-advertisement—just for friendship's or for honesty's sake.

D. SEVERO. You are unjust to yourself. To such an excess have you pushed gratitude, that you have almost sacrificed

honour and fortune to it. What more could be expected
—even of a saint? There's a limit to all things, good and
evil. He is proud and obstinate, and, however much you
may oppose him, 'tis none the less a fact that he's his
own master. If he chooses to leave your palace in a fit
of despair, for this shanty—'tis his right. I admit, my
dear boy, that it's very sad—but then, who could have
prevented it?

D. JULIAN. The world in general, if it would mind its own
business instead of tearing and rending reputations by
the movement of its tongue and the sign of its hand.
What did it matter to the public if we, fulfilling a sacred
duty, treated Ernest, I as a son, and Teodora as a
brother? Is it reason enough to assume the worst, and
trumpet scandal because a fine lad sits at my table, walks
out with my wife, and has his seat in my opera-box?
Is by chance impure love the sole supreme bond between
man and woman in this world of clay? Is there no
friendship, gratitude, sympathy, esteem, that youth and
beauty should only meet in the mire? And even
supposing that the conclusion of the fools was the right
one, is it their business to avenge me? I have my own
eyes to look after my own affairs, and to avenge my
wrongs have I not courage, steel, and my own right
hand?

D. SEVERO. Well, accepting that outsiders were wrong to
talk, did you expect me, who am of your blood and
bear your name, to hold my tongue?

D. JULIAN. By heavens, no! But you should have been
more careful. You might have told me alone of this
sorry business, and not have set flame to a conflagration
under my very roof.

D. SEVERO. I erred through excess of affection, I admit.
But while I confess that the world and I have done the
mischief—it by inventing the situation, and I by weakly
crediting, and by giving voice to the shabby innuendoes—you, Julian [*approaches him and speaks with*

tender interest], have nothing to reproach yourself with. You have the consolation of having acted throughout as a gentleman.

D. JULIAN. I cannot so easily console myself, while my heart gives shelter to that same story which my lips and my intelligence reject. I indignantly turn away from the world's calumny, and to myself I say: 'What if it should be no lie: if perchance the world should be right?' So I stand in strife between two impulses, sometimes judge, sometimes accomplice. This inward battle wears me out, Severo. Doubt increases and expands, and my heart groans, while before my bloodshot vision stretches a reddened field.

D. SEVERO. Delirium!

D. JULIAN. No, 'tis not raving. You see, I bare myself to you as a brother. Think you Ernest would have left my house if I had firmly stood in his way and opposed his crossing the threshold? If so, why does a traitorous voice keep muttering in my disturbed consciousness: ''twere wise to leave the door open to his exit, and lock it well afterwards, for the confiding man is but a poor guardian of honour's fortress.' In my heart I wish what my lips deny. 'Come back, Ernest,' aloud, and to myself 'do not come back,' and while I show him a frank front, I am a hypocrite and a coward, watchful and worn with mistrust. No, Severo, this is not to act like an honest man. [*He drops into the arm-chair beside the table in deep dejection.*]

D. SEVERO. It is how any husband would act who had a beautiful young wife to look after, especially one with a romantic temperament.

D. JULIAN. Don't speak so of Teodora. She is a mirror that our breath tarnishes by any imprudent effort to bring it to our level. It gave back the sun's pure light before the million vipers of the earth gathered to stare at it. To-day they crawl within the glass in its divine frame, but they are insubstantial shadows. My hand can wave them away, and once more you will see the clear blue of heaven.

D. SEVERO. All the better.

D. JULIAN. No, not so.

D. SEVERO. Then what the deuce do you want?

D. JULIAN. Oh, so much. I told you that this inward struggle of which I spoke is changing me to another man. Now my wife finds me always sad, always distant. I am not the man I was, and no effort will ever make me so again. Seeing me so changed, she must ask, 'Where is Julian? this is not my dear husband; what have I done to forfeit his confidence, and what shabby feeling causes this aloofness?' a shadow lies between us, ever deepening, and slowly, step by step, we move more apart. None of the old dear confidence, none of the old delightful talks; smiles frozen, tones embittered, in me through unjust resentment, in her through tearful grief,—I wounded in my love, and she, by my hand, wounded in her woman's dignity. There's how we stand.

D. SEVERO. Then you stand upon the verge of perdition. If you see your position so plainly, why don't you remedy it?

D. JULIAN. 'Tis of no use. I know I am unjust to doubt her, nay, worse still. I don't doubt her now. But who will say that, I losing little by little, and he gaining as steadily, the lie of to-day will not to-morrow be truth? [*He seizes Don Severo by the arm, and speaks with voluble earnestness and increasing bitterness.*] I, jealous, sombre, unjust and hard, he noble and generous, resigned and inalterably sweet-natured, with that halo of martyrdom which, in the eyes of women, sits so becomingly on the brow of a brave and handsome youth. Is it not clear that his is the better part, and that my loss is his

gain? while I can do nothing to alter the injustice of it.
You see it, too? And if the ignoble talk of the town
should compel those two to treason, though they may
now truthfully assert: 'we are not lovers,' the force of
repetition of the word may eventually drive them to
the fact.

D. SEVERO. If that's how you feel about it, Julian, I think
the safest thing would be to let Ernest carry out his
project.

D. JULIAN. That I've come to prevent.

D. SEVERO. Then you are insane. He purposes to go to
Buenos Ayres. Nothing could be better. Let him go—
in a sailing vessel, fresh wind to his sail, and good
speed.

D. JULIAN. Do you wish me to show myself so miserably
ungrateful and jealous before Teodora? Don't you
know, Severo, that a woman may despise a lover and
love him still, but not so a husband? Contempt is his
dishonour. You would not have my wife follow the unhappy exile across the ocean with sad regrets? And I,
should I see the trace of a tear upon her cheek, the mere
thought that it might be for Ernest would drive me to
strangle her in my arms. [*Speaks with rancour and
rage.*]

D. SEVERO. What is it then you do want?

D. JULIAN. I must suffer. The care of unravelling the
knot belongs to the world that conceived the drama
solely by looking at us,—so fertile is its glance for good
and ill.

D. SEVERO. [*Moving back.*] I think somebody is coming.

SERVANT. [*From without, not seen on the stage.*] Don
Ernest cannot be much later. [*Enter Pepito.*]

SCENE III

Don Julian, Don Severo, and Pepito.

D. SEVERO. You here?

PEPITO [*Aside.*] By Jove, I see they know all about it. [*Aloud.*] We are all here. How do you do, uncle? How do, father? [*Aside.*] Easy. They know what's in the wind. [*Aloud.*] What brings you?—but I suppose you are looking for Ernest.

D. SEVERO. What else could bring us here?

D. JULIAN. I daresay you know what this madman is up to?

PEPITO. What he's up to! Well, yes—rather. I know as much as another.

D. SEVERO. And it's to-morrow?

PEPITO. No, to-morrow he is going away, so it must be to-day.

D. JULIAN. [*Surprised.*] What do you say?

PEPITO. That's what Pepe Uceda told me last night at the club. He is Nebreda's second, so he ought to know. But why do you stare so oddly? Didn't you know——

D. JULIAN. [*Hastily covering his brother's movement.*] Everything.

D. SEVERO. We——

D. JULIAN. [*Aside.*] Hold your tongue, Severo.—He starts to-morrow, and to-day he stakes his life—and we are here, of course, to prevent both, the duel and the departure. [*Don Julian makes it evident that he is only sounding Pepito's knowledge of facts, and that he is only aware of the pending departure.*]

D. SEVERO. What duel?

D. JULIAN. [*Aside to Severo.*] I know nothing about it, but I shall presently.

PEPITO. [*Aside.*] Come, I haven't been such a duffer after all.

D. JULIAN. [*Speaking with an air of certainty.*] We know there is a viscount——

PEPITO. Yes.

D. JULIAN. With whom Ernest proposes to fight—a certain trustworthy person has informed us, who was at once apprised of it. They say 'tis a serious matter [*Pepito nods*], a disgraceful quarrel in the presence of several witnesses [*Pepito nods again*]—the lie direct, and a deluge of bad language——

PEPITO. [*Interrupts excitedly, glad of his more accurate information.*] Language indeed!—a blow bigger than a monument.

D. SEVERO. On which side?

PEPITO. Ernest struck the viscount.

D. JULIAN. Of course Ernest struck the viscount. I thought you knew that, Severo. The viscount insulted him. Patience is not the lad's strong point—hence the blow.

PEPITO. Exactly.

D. JULIAN. [*Confidently.*] I told you we knew the whole story. [*Then anxiously.*] The affair is serious?

PEPITO. Most serious. I don't like discussing it, but since you know so much, there is no need for further mystery.

D. JULIAN. None whatever. [*He approaches Pepito eagerly.*]

PEPITO. [*After a pause, adopts an ominous air to announce bad news.*] It is a matter of life and death. [*Looks round triumphantly. Don Julian and Don Severo start.*] The viscount is neither a chicken nor a skulk. He can handle a sword.

D. JULIAN. And the quarrel? What was it? Nebreda is supposed to be——

PEPITO. It was hardly a quarrel. I'll tell you the facts. [*Both men draw near eagerly.*] Ernest, you know, means to leave Madrid to-morrow, and take passage in the *Cid* lying in Cadiz. Luiz Alcaráz had promised him a letter of introduction, and the poor fellow went off to meet him at the *café* and get it, with the best of intentions. Luiz wasn't there, so he waited. Some of the frequenters of Alcaráz's table, who did not know him, were in the full swing of glorious slander, and did not notice his clenched teeth. A name mentioned meant a reputation blasted. Broad-handed, ready-tongued, every living soul passed in their review. In this asylum of charity, in the midst of more smoke than an express train emits, between lifted glass and dropped cigarette ashes, with here and there a lump of sugar, the marble was converted for the nonce into a dissecting-table: each woman dishonoured, another glass of the old tap: a shout of laughter for each tippler's cut. In four clippings these lads left reputations ragged and the ladies rent to tatters. Yet what did it all come to? They but echoed society at a *café*-table. I don't say all this for myself, nor think it, but 'twas how Ernest spoke when he recounted the quarrel to me.

D. JULIAN. Well, make an end of it.

PEPITO. The end of it is, that between name and name, there was mention of one that Ernest could not endure. 'Who dares to ridicule an honourable man?' he shouts. Somebody retorts: 'a lady,' and names a woman. His head was instantly on fire, and he flings himself upon Nebreda. The poor viscount fell like a ninepin, and there you have an Agramante's camp. The day's business is now a duel—in a room somewhere—I don't know where.

D. JULIAN. [*Seizing his arms.*] The man was I!

PEPITO. Sir?

D. JULIAN. And Teodora the woman? How have we fallen—she, myself, our love? [*Sits down and covers his face with both hands.*]

SEVERO. What have you done, you blockhead!

PEPITO. Didn't he say he knew all about it? and I naturally believed him.

D. JULIAN. Dishonoured, dishonoured!

SEVERO. [*Approaching him.*] Julian, my dear fellow.

D. JULIAN. It is true. I ought to be calm, I know. But what heart can I have when faith is gone? [*Seizes his brother's hand.*] Just heaven! Why are we so disgraced? What reason have they to turn and throw mud at us? No matter. I know my duty as a gentleman. I can count on you, Severo?

SEVERO. On me? Till death, Julian. [*They shake hands cordially.*]

JULIAN. [*To Pepito.*] The duel?

PEPITO. For three o'clock.

JULIAN. [*Aside.*] I'll kill him—yes, kill him. Come. [*To Severo.*]

SEVERO. Whither?

D. JULIAN. To look for this viscount.

SEVERO. Do you mean——?

D. JULIAN. I mean to do what I ought and can to avenge myself and save Don Juan of Acedo's son. Who are the seconds? [*To Pepito.*]

PEPITO. Alcaráz and Rueda.

D. JULIAN. I know them both. Let him stay here [*pointing to Pepito*], so that in the event of Ernest's return——

SEVERO. Of course.

D. JULIAN. [*To Pepito.*] Without arousing his suspicion, find out where the duel takes place.

SEVERO. You hear.

D. JULIAN. [*To his brother.*] Come.

SEVERO. What's the matter with you, Julian?

D. JULIAN. 'Tis a long while since I've felt so overjoyed. [*Catches Severo's arm feverishly.*]

SEVERO. The deuce! overjoyed! You're beside yourself.

D. JULIAN. I shall meet that fellow.

SEVERO. Nebreda?

D. JULIAN. Yes. Observe, until to-day calumny was impalpable. There was no seizing its shape. I have now discovered it, and it has taken a human form. There it is at hand, in the person of a viscount. Swallowing blood and gall for the past three months—the devil!—and now—fancy, face to face—he and I!
[*Exeunt Don Julian and Don Severo.*]

SCENE IV

PEPITO. Well, here we are in a nice fix, and all for nothing! However, in spite of my uncle's belief, it was little short of madness to leave a resplendent creature under the same roof and in continual contact with a handsome fellow like Ernest, with a soul on fire, or given to romanticism. He swears there's nothing in it, and that his feeling for her is pure affection, that

he loves her like a sister, and that my uncle is a
father to him. But I am a sly fox, and, young as I
am, I know a thing or two of this world. I've no faith
in this sort of relations, when the brother is young
and the sister is beautiful, and brotherhood between
them a fiction. But suppose it were as he says, all
square. What do outsiders know about that? Nobody
is under any obligation to think the best of his fellows.
The pair are seen everywhere together, and, seeing
them, haven't their neighbours a right to talk? No,
swears Ernest. *We hardly ever went out alone.* Once,
perhaps? That's enough. If a hundred persons saw
them on that occasion, it is quite the same as if they
had been seen in public a hundred times. Good Lord!
How are you going to confront all the witnesses to
prove whether it was once or often they chose to give
an airing to this pure sympathy and brotherly love?
'Tis absurd—neither just nor reasonable. What we
see we may mention—'tis no lie to say it. 'I saw
them once,' says one, 'and I,' another. One and one
make two. 'And I also'—that makes three. And
then a fourth, and a fifth, and so, summing which, you
soon enough reach infinity. We see because we look,
and our senses are there to help us to pass the time,
without any thought of our neighbour. He must
look out for himself, and remember that, if he shuns
the occasion, calumny and peril will shun him. [*Pause.*]
And take notice that I admit the purity of the affection,
and this makes it so serious a matter. Now, in my
opinion, the man who could be near Teodora, and not
fall in love with her, must be a stone. He may be
learned and philosophical, and know physics and
mathematics, but he has a body like another, and
she's there with a divine one, and, body of Bacchus!
that's sufficient to found an accusation on. Ah! if
these walls could speak. If Ernest's private thoughts,
scattered here, could take tangible form! By Jove!
what's this? An empty frame, and beside it Don
Julian's likeness in its fellow. Teodora was there,

the pendant of my respected uncle. Why has she disappeared? To avoid temptation? [*Sits down at the table.*] If that's the reason—it's bad. And still worse if the portrait has left its frame for a more honourable place near his heart. Come forth, suspected imps that float about, and weave invisible meshes. Ruthlessly denounce this mystic philosopher. [*Looks about the table and sees the open Dante.*] Here's another. I never come here but I find this divine book open on Ernest's table. The Divine Comedy! His favourite poem, and I note that he seems never to get beyond the Francesca page. I conceive two explanations of the fact. Either the fellow never reads it, or he never reads any other. But there's a stain, like a tear-drop. My faith! what mysteries and abysses! And what a difficult thing it is to be married and live tranquilly. A paper half burnt—[*picks it up*]—there's still a morsel left. [*Goes over to the balcony trying to read it. At this moment Ernest enters, and stands watching him.*]

SCENE V

Pepito and Ernest.

ERNEST. What are you looking at?

PEPITO. Hulloa! Ernest. Only a paper I caught on the wing. The wind blew it away.

ERNEST. [*Takes it and returns it after a short inspection.*] I don't remember what it is.

PEPITO. Verses. You may remember [*reads with difficulty*] 'The flame that consumes me.' [*Aside.*] *Devora* rhymes with *Teodora*.

ERNEST. It is nothing important.

PEPITO. No, nothing. [*Throws away the paper.*]

ERNEST. That worthless bit of paper is a symbol of our life—a few sobs of sorrow, and a little flake of ashes.

PEPITO. Then they were verses?

ERNEST. Yes. When I've nothing better to do, sometimes—my pen runs away with me—I write them at night.

PEPITO. And to prick enthusiasm, and get into harness, you seek inspiration in the master's book.

ERNEST. It would seem——

PEPITO. Say no more. 'Tis truly a gigantic work. The episode of Francesca. [*Pointing to the page.*]

ERNEST. [*Ironically and impatiently.*] You can't guess wrong to-day.

PEPITO. Not entirely, by Jove. Here, where the book is open, I find something I can't guess, and you must explain it to me. Reading a love-tale together to pass the time, we are told that Francesca and Paolo reached that part where the gallant author, proving himself no amateur in the business, sings the loves of Launcelot and Queen Guinevere. The match fell pat. The kiss in the book was repeated by the passionate youth on the girl's mouth. And at this point of the story, with rare skill and sublime truth, the Florentine poet tells us what happens. [*Points to the line.*] But this is what I do not understand. *Galeoto was the book they were reading, and they read no more.* They stopped reading? That's easy enough to understand. But this Galeoto, tell me where he comes in, and who was he? You ought to know, since he has given his name to the play that is to make you famous. Let me see. [*Takes up the MS. and examines it.*]

ERNEST. Galeoto was the go-between for the Queen and Launcelot and in all loves the *third* may be truthfully nicknamed Galeoto, above all when we wish to suggest an ugly word without shocking an audience.

PEPITO. I see, but have we no Spanish word to express it?

ERNEST. We have one, quite suitable and expressive enough. 'Tis an office that converts desires into ducats, overcomes scruples, and is fed upon the affections. It has a name, but to use it would be putting a fetter upon myself, forcing myself to express what, after all, I would leave unsaid. [*Takes the MS. from Pepito and flings it upon the table.*] Each especial case, I have remarked, has its own especial go-between. Sometimes it is the entire social mass that is Galeoto. It then unconsciously exercises the office under the influence of a vice of quite another aspect, but so dexterously does it work against honour and modesty that no greater Galeoto can ever be found. Let a man and woman live happily, in tranquil and earnest fulfilment of their separate duties. Nobody minds them, and they float along at ease. But God be praised, this is a state of things that does not last long in Madrid. One morning somebody takes the trouble to notice them, and from that moment, behold society engaged in the business, without aim or object, on the hunt for hidden frailty and impurity. Then it pronounces and judges, and there is no logic that can convince it, nor living man who can hope to persuade it, and the honestest has not a rag of honour left. And the terrible thing is, that while it begins in error it generally ends in truth. The atmosphere is so dense, misery so envelops the pair, such is the press and torrent of slander, that they unconsciously seek one another, unite lovelessly, drift toward their fall, and adore each other until death. The world was the stumbling-stone of virtue, and made clear the way for shame—was Galeoto and—[*aside*] stay! what mad thought inflames me!

PEPITO. [*Aside.*] If that's the way he discourses to Teodora, heaven help poor Don Julian. [*Aloud.*] I suppose last night's verses dealt with the subject.

ERNEST. Yes, they did.

PEPITO. How can you waste your time so coolly, and sit there so calm, doing nothing, when in another hour you will be measuring swords with Nebreda, who, for all his dandy's cane, is a man when put upon his mettle? Wouldn't it be saner and wiser to practise fencing instead of expounding questions of verse and rhyme? You look so mighty cool that I almost doubt if you regard your meeting with the viscount as serious.

ERNEST. No,—for a good reason. If I kill him, the world gains; if he kill me, I gain.

PEPITO. Well, that's good.

ERNEST. Don't say any more about it.

PEPITO. [*Aside.*] Now I must warily find out. [*Approaches him and speaks in a low voice.*] Is it for to-day?

ERNEST. Yes, to-day.

PEPITO. Outside the town?

ERNEST, No, there's no time for that. Besides, we wish to keep it quiet.

PEPITO. In a house, then?

ERNEST. So I proposed.

PEPITO. Where?

ERNEST. Upstairs. [*Speaks with cold indifference.*] There's a room unlet upstairs, with a side window, through which nobody can look. Under the circumstances it's better than a field, and will be had for a handful of silver.

PEPITO. And now all you need——

ERNEST. The swords!

PEPITO. I hear voices outside. Somebody is coming— the seconds?

ERNEST. May be.

PEPITO. It sounds like a woman's voice. [*Approaches the door.*]

ERNEST. [*Approaching also.*] But who's keeping them?

SCENE VI.

Ernest, Pepito, and Servant.

SERVANT. [*Mysteriously.*] Somebody wants to see you, sir.

ERNEST. Who?

SERVANT. A lady.

ERNEST. How extraordinary!

PEPITO. [*Aside to servant.*] What does she want?

SERVANT. [*To Pepito.*] She is crying.

PEPITO. [*Aloud.*] Is she young?

SERVANT. Really, sir, I can't say. It's very dark outside, and the lady's face is so thickly veiled that the devil himself couldn't tell what she's like, and she speaks so low you can't even hear her.

ERNEST. Who can she be?

PEPITO. Who could want to see you?

ERNEST. I cannot think.

PEPITO. [*Aside.*] This is startling. [*Takes up his hat and holds out his hand.*] Well, I'll leave you in peace. Good-bye and good luck. [*To the servant.*] What are you waiting for, you booby?

SERVANT. For orders to show the lady in.

PEPITO. In such a case 'tis your business to anticipate

them. And afterwards, until the veiled one has departed, you mustn't let any one in unless the sky were falling.

SERVANT. Then I am to show her in?

ERNEST. Yes. [*To Pepito at the door.*] Good-bye.

PEPITO. Good-bye, Ernest. [*Exeunt servant and Pepito.*]

ERNEST. A lady? on what pretext? What does this mean? [*Enter Teodora, thickly veiled; she stands without approaching.*] Ah, there she is!

SCENE VII

Teodora and Ernest, she behind not daring to advance, he turned toward her.

ERNEST. You desire to speak to me, madam? Kindly be seated. [*Offers her a chair.*]

TEODORA. [*Unveiling.*] Forgive me, Ernest.

ERNEST. Teodora!

TEODORA. I am wrong to come—am I not?

ERNEST. [*Abruptly and stammering.*] I can't say—since I don't know to what I owe this honour. But what am I saying? Alas! Here, in my rooms, madam, reverence attends you, than which you cannot find a greater [*with devotion*]. But what wrong can you possibly fear here, lady?

TEODORA. None—and there was a time—but that *once* is for ever past. No thought of doubt or fear was then. I might have crossed any room on your arm without blush or fluttering pulse. But now! They tell me that you are starting for America to-morrow—and I—yes—like those who go away—perhaps not to return—it is so sad to lose a friend!—before Julian—before the whole world—thinking only of our affection—I myself, Ernest, would have held out my arms to you—in farewell.

ERNEST. [*Starts and quickly restrains himself.*] Oh, Teodora!

TEODORA. But now I suppose it is not the same thing. There is a gulf between us.

ERNEST. You are right, madam. We may no longer care for one another, be no longer brother and sister. The mutual touch of palm would leave our hands unclean. 'Tis all for ever past. What we have now to learn is to hate one another.

TEODORA. [*In naïve consternation.*] Hate! surely not!

ERNEST. Have I used that word—and to you! poor child!

TEODORA. Yes.

ERNEST. Don't heed me. If you needed my life, and the occasion offered itself, claim it, Teodora, for, to give my life for you would be——[*with passion*] it would be my duty. [*With a sudden change of voice. Pause.*] Hate! if my lips pronounced the word, I was thinking of the misery,—I was thinking of the injury I have unwittingly wrought one to whom I owe so much. Yes, you, Teodora, must hate me—but I—ah, no!

TEODORA. [*Sadly.*] They have made me shed tears enough; yes, you are right in that, Ernest [*with tenderness*], but you I do not accuse. Who could condemn or blame you for all this talk? You have nothing to do with the venomous solicitude with which evil minds honour us, nor with poor Julian's clouded temper. It is sorrow that makes him restive, and his suffering wounds me, for I know that it springs from doubt of my devotion.

ERNEST. That is what I cannot understand [*angrily*], and in him less than in another. It is what drives me wild: by the living God, I protest it is not worthy of pity, and there is no excuse for it. That the man should exist who could doubt a woman like you!

TEODORA. Poor fellow, he pays a heavy price for his savage distrust.

ERNEST. [*Horrified to find he has been blaming Don Julian to Teodora.*] What have I said? I don't accuse him—no—I meant—— [*He hastens to exculpate Don Julian and modify his former words.*] Anybody might feel the same, that is, if he were very much in love. In our earthly egoism, don't we doubt the very God in heaven? And the owner of a treasure jealously watches it as gold, and cannot but fear for it. I, too, in his place, would be full of doubt,—yes—even of my own brother. [*Speaks with increasing fervour, and again restrains himself, perceiving that he is on the brink of a peril he would avoid. Teodora hears voices outside and rushes to the door.*]

ERNEST. Whither are you leading me, rebel heart? What depth have I stirred? I accuse the world of calumny, and would now prove it right.

TEODORA. Do you hear? Somebody is coming.

ERNEST. [*Following her.*] It is hardly two o'clock. Can it be ——?

TEODORA. [*With terror.*] It is Julian's voice.—He is coming in!

ERNEST. No, they have prevented him.

TEODORA [*Turns to Ernest, still frightened.*] If it were Julian? [*Moves towards the bedroom door. Ernest detains her respectfully.*]

ERNEST. Should it be he, stay here. Loyalty is our shield. Were it one of those who distrust us—then there, Teodora. [*Points to the door.*] Ah, nobody. [*Listening.*]

TEODORA. How my heart throbs!

ERNEST. You need not be afraid. The person who

wanted to come in has gone away—or it was an illusion. For God's sake, Teodora——! [*Advances up the stage.*]

TEODORA. I had so much to say to you, Ernest, and the time has passed so quickly.

ERNEST. The time has flown.

TEODORA. I wanted——

ERNEST. Teodora, pray forgive me—but is it prudent? If any one came in—and, indeed, I fear some one will.

TEODORA. That is why I came—to prevent it.

ERNEST. So that ——?

TEODORA. I know everything, and I am stricken with horror at the thought that blood should be shed on my account. My head is on fire, my heart is bursting. [*Strikes her breast.*]

ERNEST. It is the affront that burns and shames you until my hand has struck at Nebreda's life. He wanted mud! Well, let him have it stained with blood.

TEODORA. You would kill him?

ERNEST. Certainly. [*Represses Teodora's movement of supplication.*] You can dispose of me in all else but in this one thing. Do not ask me to feel compassion for a man whose insult I remember.

TEODORA. [*Prayerfully, with a sob.*] For my sake!

ERNEST. For your sake?

TEODORA. It would be such a horrible scandal.

ERNEST. That is possible.

TEODORA. You can say it so coolly, and not endeavour to avoid it, not even when it is I who implore you!

ERNEST. I cannot avoid it, but I can chastise it: so I

think and say, and this is my business. Others will look for the insult, I for the punishment.

TEODORA. [*Coming nearer and speaking softly, as if afraid of her own voice.*] And Julian?

ERNEST. Well?

TEODORA. If he were to know about it?

ERNEST. He will know about it.

TEODORA. What will he say?

ERNEST. What?

TEODORA. That only my husband, the man who loves me, has a right to defend me.

ERNEST. Every honourable man has the right to defend a lady. He may not even know her, be neither a friend, nor a relative, nor a lover. It is enough for him to hear a woman insulted. Why do I fight this duel? Why do I defend her? Because I heard the calumny. Because I am myself. Who is so base as to give his protection by scale and measure? Was I not there? Then whoever it was—I or another—who was first on the scene——

TEODORA. [*Listens eagerly, dominated by him, and holds out her hand to him.*] This is noble and honourable, and worthy of you, Ernest [*then restrains herself and moves backward*]. But it leaves Julian humiliated [*with conviction*].

ERNEST. He? humiliated!

TEODORA. Most surely.

ERNEST. Why?

TEODORA. For no reason whatever.

ERNEST. Who will say so?

TEODORA. Everybody.

ERNEST. But wherefore?

TEODORA. When the world hears of the affront, and learns that it was not my husband who avenged me, and above all [*drops her eyes ashamed*] that it was you who took his place—have we not then a new scandal topping the old?

ERNEST. [*Convinced but protests.*] If one had always to think of what people will say, by Heaven there would be no manner or means of living then!

TEODORA. It is so, nevertheless.

ERNEST. Just so. 'Tis horrible.

TEODORA. Then yield.

ERNEST. Impossible.

TEODORA. I beseech you.

ERNEST. No. Looking into the matter, as nobody can know what will happen, it is better that I should face Nebreda. For, after all, if the fellow lack a sense of honour, he can use a sword.

TEODORA. [*Wounded and humiliated in the protection Ernest seems to offer Don Julian.*] My husband is not lacking in courage.

ERNEST. Fatality again! Either I have expressed myself ill, or you do not understand me. I know his worth. But when a desperate injury lies between men of courage, who knows what may happen? which of them may fall, and which may kill? And if this man's sword must strike Don Julian or Ernest, can you doubt which it ought to be? [*Questions her with sad sincerity.*]

TEODORA. [*In anguish.*] You!—oh, no—not that either.

ERNEST. Why? If it is my fate? Nobody loses by my death, and I lose still less.

TEODORA. For Heaven's sake, do not say that [*Barely able to repress her sobs.*]

ERNEST. What do I leave behind me? Neither friendship

nor strong love. What woman is there to follow my corpse shedding a lover's tears?

TEODORA. Last night I prayed for you—and you say that nobody——I could not bear you to die. [*Vehemently.*]

ERNEST. Ah, we pray for any one; we only weep for one. [*With passion.*]

TEODORA. [*Startled.*] Ernest!

ERNEST. [*Terrified by his own words.*] What!

TEODORA. [*Moving further away.*] Nothing.

ERNEST. [*Also moving away and looking nervously down.*] I told you a little while ago I was half mad. Do not heed me. [*Pause. Both remain silent and pensive, at some distance, not looking at each other.*]

TEODORA. [*Starting and glancing anxiously down the stage.*] Again!

ERNEST. [*Following her movement.*] Somebody has come.

TEODORA. They are trying to get in.

ERNEST [*Listening.*] There can be no doubt of it. There, Teodora. [*Points to the bedroom door.*]

TEODORA. My honour is my shield.

ERNEST. But it is not your husband.

TEODORA. Not Julian?

ERNEST. [*Leading her to the door.*] No.

TEODORA. I hoped—— [*Detains him with an air of supplication.*] Will you give up this duel?

ERNEST. Give it up? When I've struck him!

TEODORA. I didn't know that. [*Despairingly, but understands that nothing can be done.*] Then fly.

ERNEST. I fly!

TEODORA. For my sake, for his sake—for God's sake!

ERNEST. [*Despairingly.*] You must loathe me to propose such a thing to me. Never!

TEODORA. One word only. Are they coming for you now?

ERNEST. It is not yet time.

TEODORA. Swear it to me.

ERNEST. Yes, Teodora. And you—say you don't hate me.

TEODORA. Never.

PEPITO. [*Outside.*] Nothing. I must see him.

ERNEST. Quickly.

TEODORA. Yes. [*Hides in the bedroom.*]

PEPITO. Why do you prevent me?

ERNEST. Ah, calumny is working to make the lie truth.

SCENE VIII

Ernest and Pepito, without his hat, exhibiting strong excitement.

PEPITO. Go to the devil—I will go in—Ernest.

ERNEST. What has happened?

PEPITO. I hardly know how to tell you—yet I must——

ERNEST. Speak.

PEPITO. My head is in a whirl. Christ above, who would think——

ERNEST. Quickly. A clear account of what has happened.

PEPITO. What has happened? A great misfortune. Don Julian heard of the duel. He came here to look for you, and you were out. He went away to find the seconds, and marched them off to Nebreda's house.

ERNEST. Nebreda's! How?

PEPITO. The Lord send you sense. Don Julian's way, of course, who makes short work of convention and the will of others.

ERNEST. Go on——

PEPITO. [*Going to the door.*] They're coming, I believe.

ERNEST. Who?

PEPITO. They—they're carrying Don Julian.

ERNEST. You terrify me. Explain at once. [*Catches his arm violently, and drags him forward.*]

PEPITO. He compelled him to fight. There was no way out of it. The viscount cried: 'Very well, between us two.' It was settled it should take place here. Don Julian came upstairs. Your servant sent him away, protesting you were engaged with a lady, and swearing nobody could enter.

ERNEST. And then?

PEPITO. Don Julian went downstairs muttering 'better so. I have the day's work for myself.' And he, my father, Nebreda and the seconds came back together, and went upstairs.

ERNEST. They fought?

PEPITO. Furiously, as men fight when their intent is deadly, and their enemy's heart is within reach of the sword's point.

ERNEST. And Don Julian! No—it must be a lie.

PEPITO. Here they are.

ERNEST. Silence. Tell me who it is, but speak softly.

PEPITO. There. [*Enter Don Julian, Don Severo, and Rueda. The two men support Don Julian, who is badly wounded.*]

ERNEST. Heaven preserve us!

SCENE IX

Ernest, Pepito, Don Julian, Don Severo, and Rueda.

ERNEST. Don Julian! my friend, my father, my benefactor! [*Hurries excitedly toward him, and speaks brokenly.*]

D. JULIAN [*Weakly.*] Ernest!

ERNEST. Oh, wretched I!

SEVERO. Quick, come away.

ERNEST. Father!

SEVERO. He is fainting with pain.

ERNEST. For my sake!

JULIAN. It is not so.

ERNEST. Through me—pardon! [*Takes Don Julian's hand and bends on one knee before him.*]

JULIAN. No need to ask it, lad. You did your duty, and I did mine.

SEVERO. A couch. [*Loosens his hold of Don Julian, and Pepito takes his place.*]

PEPITO. [*Pointing to the bedroom.*] Let us carry him in there.

ERNEST. [*Shouting terribly.*] Nebreda!

SEVERO. Let there be an end to folly. Is it your intention to kill him outright?

ERNEST. [*With frenzy.*] Folly, oh, we'll see. I have two to avenge now. It is my right. [*Rushes down the stage.*]

SEVERO. [*Moving to the right*]. We'll take him into your

room and lay him on the bed. [*Ernest wheels round in terror.*]

ERNEST. Where?

SEVERO. In here.

PEPITO. Yes.

ERNEST. No. [*Strides back, and stands before the door. The group are on the point of lifting Don Julian, desist, and stare at Ernest in indignant surprise.*]

SEVERO. You forbid it?

PEPITO. Are you mad?

SEVERO. Back: can't you see he is dying?

D. JULIAN. What is it? He doesn't wish it? [*Raises himself and looks at Ernest in distrust and fear.*]

RUEDA. I don't understand it.

PEPITO. Nor I.

ERNEST. He is dying—and implores me—and doubts me—father!

SEVERO. Come, we must. [*Pushes open the door above Ernest's shoulder. Teodora is discovered.*]

ERNEST. My God!

SEVERO and PEPITO. She!

RUEDA. A woman!

TEODORA. [*Coming forward to her husband and embracing him*] Julian!

D. JULIAN. Who is it? [*Pushes her away to stare at her, drags himself to his feet with a violent effort, and shakes himself free of all aid.*] Teodora! [*Falls lifeless to the ground.*]

ACT III

The same decoration as first act: an arm-chair instead of a sofa. It is night; a lighted lamp stands on the table.

SCENE I

Pepito listening at the door on the right, then comes back into the middle of the stage.

PEPITO. The crisis is past at last. I hear nothing. Poor Don Julian! He's in a sad way. His life hangs in the balance: on one side death awaits him, and on the other another death, that of the soul, of honour—either abyss deeper than hopeless love. The devil! All this tragedy is making me more sentimental than that fellow with his plays and verses. The tune of disaster, scandal, death, treason, and disgrace, hums in my brain. By Jove, what a day, and what a night! and the worst is yet to come. Well, it certainly was madness to move him in his condition; but when once my uncle gets an idea into his head, there's no reasoning with him. And, after all, he was right. No honourable man, in his place, could have stayed, and he is a man of spirit. Who is coming? my mother, I believe—yes. [*Enter Doña Mercedes.*]

SCENE II

Pepito and Doña Mercedes.

MERCEDES. Where's Severo?

PEPITO. He has not left my uncle for a moment. I had

no idea he was so attached to him. If what I fear should happen——

MERCEDES. How is your uncle?

PEPITO. He suffers greatly, but says nothing. Sometimes he calls out 'Teodora' in a low harsh voice, and sometimes 'Ernest'; and then he tugs violently at the sheets, and lies quiet again as a statue, staring vacantly into space. Now his brow is bathed in the cold sweat of death, and then fever seizes him. He sits up in bed, listens attentively, and shouts that *he* and *she* are waiting for him. He tries to jump out of bed to rush at them, and all my father's entreaties and commands barely suffice to restrain him or soothe him. There's no quieting him. Anger races hot through his veins, and thought is a flame. It is shocking, mother, to see the bitter way his lips contract, and how his fingers close in a vice, with head all wild, and pupils dilated as though they drank in with yearning and despair every shadow that floats around the chamber.

MERCEDES. How does your father bear it?

PEPITO. He groans and breathes of vengeance. He, too, mutters the names of Teodora and Ernest. I hope to God he will not meet either, for if he should, small chance there is of restraining his fury.

MERCEDES. Your father is a good man.

PEPITO. Yes, but with a temper——

MERCEDES. It is not easily aroused, however. But when he has cause——

PEPITO. With all due respect, he's then a very tiger.

MERCEDES. Only when provoked.

PEPITO. I don't know about other occasions, but this time he certainly has provocation enough. And Teodora?

MERCEDES. She is upstairs. She wanted to come down —and cried—like a Magdalen.

PEPITO. Already! Repentant or erring?

MERCEDES. Don't speak so. Unhappy girl, she is but a child.

PEPITO. Who, innocent and candid, sweet and pure and meek, kills Don Julian. So that, if I am to accept your word, and regard her as a child, and such is her work on the edge of infancy, we may pray God in his mercy to guard us from her when she shall have put on years.

MERCEDES. She is hardly to be blamed. The infamy lies with your fine friend—he of the dramas, the poet and dreamer. He it is who is the culprit.

PEPITO. I don't deny it.

MERCEDES. Where is he?

PEPITO. Where is he? At this moment racing about the streets and public places, flying from his conscience, and unable to get away from it.

MERCEDES. He has a conscience?

PEPITO. So it would seem.

MERCEDES. Oh, what a tragedy!

PEPITO. A misfortune!

MERCEDES. Such a deception!

PEPITO. A cruel one.

MERCEDES. What shocking treason!

PEPITO. Unparalleled.

MERCEDES. Poor Julian!

PEPITO. Melancholy fate! [*Enter servant.*]

SCENE III

Doña Mercedes, Pepito, and servant.

SERVANT. Don Ernest.

MERCEDES. He dares——

PEPITO. This is too much.

SERVANT. I thought——

PEPITO. You had no business to think anything.

SERVANT. He is only passing. There is a cab waiting, so——

PEPITO. What are we to do?

MERCEDES. Let him come in. [*Exit servant.*]

PEPITO. I'll give him his dismissal.

MERCEDES. Do it cleverly.

SCENE IV

Doña Mercedes, Pepito, and Ernest. Doña Mercedes seated in the arm-chair, Pepito standing, and Ernest behind, whom neither salute nor look at.

ERNEST. [*Aside.*] Hostile silence, anger, and contempt. Through no fault of my own, I now appear to them a prodigy of evil and insolence, and they all despise me.

PEPITO. Listen to me, Ernest. [*Turns round to him and speaks in a hard voice.*]

ERNEST. Well.

PEPITO. I have to tell you——

ERNEST. To go away, perhaps.

PEPITO. [*Changing his tone.*] Good heavens! What a notion! I only—wanted to ask you—if it is true [*hunts for something to say*] that you afterwards—the viscount, you know?

ERNEST. [*Gloomily looking away.*] Yes.

PEPITO. How did it happen?

ERNEST. I ran downstairs—half mad—I found them—we went upstairs again—locked the door. Two men—two witnesses—two swords—and afterwards—I hardly know what happened. Swords clashed—there was a cry—a thrust—blood spouted—an assassin stood—and a man lay stretched on the ground.

PEPITO. The devil! Sharp work. Did you hear, mother?

MERCEDES. More blood shed.

PEPITO. Nebreda deserved it.

ERNEST. [*Approaching her.*] Mercedes, for pity's sake—one word—Don Julian? How is he? If you could know what my anguish is—my sorrow—what do they say?

MERCEDES. That the wound, since his removal, is mortal, and it would be worse for him if you went near the bed of suffering and death. Leave this house.

ERNEST. I must see him.

MERCEDES. Go, instantly.

ERNEST. I will not.

PEPITO. What insolence!

ERNEST. It is befitting. [*To Pepito.*] Pardon me, madam [*turning respectfully to Mercedes*]; you see I am achieving the general opinion of me.

MERCEDES. For pity's sake, Ernest——

ERNEST. Listen, Mercedes. When a man such as I am is abused, and for no reason on earth treated as a blackguard, and finds himself snared, with crime thrust upon him, 'tis indeed a perilous case,—for others rather than for himself. I, in this fierce struggle with miserable fate, have lost honour, friendship and love, and have now nothing more to lose but the shabby shreds of an insipid and dreary existence. I have come here solely to know if there is any hope—only for that—and then—but you cannot deny me so slight a consolation? [*Pleading.*] One word!

MERCEDES. Very well. They say—that he is better.

ERNEST. True? You are not deceiving me? You are sure—quite sure? Oh! you are merciful, you are kind. It is true, quite true! May God spare him! Not his death. Let him live and be happy once more; let him forgive me and embrace me once again! Only let me see him. [*Falls into the arm-chair beside the table sobbing, and covers his face with his hands. Pause.*]

MERCEDES. If your father should hear—if he should come out. Courage, Ernest, be sensible. [*Doña Mercedes and Pepito endeavour to screen Ernest.*]

PEPITO. These nervous creatures are terrible. They sob and kill in the same breath.

ERNEST. If you see me crying, while sobs shake my throat in an hysterical convulsion, and I seem as weak as a child, or a woman, believe me, it is not for myself, but for him—for her—for their lost happiness, for this indelible blot upon their name,—for the affront I am the cause of, in return for all their love and kindness. It is not my fault, but my utter misfortune. That is why I weep. My God, if I could wipe out this wretched past with tears, I would gladly weep away my blood to the last drop.

MERCEDES. Silence, I implore!

PEPITO. There, we will discuss tears and sorrows another time.

ERNEST. If everybody else is discussing them to-day, why should we too not speak of them? The whole town is astir and on tiptoe with excitement. It has swallowed up, devoured and blighted three reputations, three names, three persons, and floated them on the froth of laughter and a wave of degrading chatter down the straits of human misery, into the social abyss of shame, where for ever lie engulfed the conscience, and fame, and future of the unfortunates.

MERCEDES. Not so loud, Ernest.

ERNEST. Why? since the others are not murmurs, but voices, that thunder through the air? The tragic event is known all over the town, and each one has his own way of telling it. Wonderful! everything is known except the truth. 'Tis fatality. [*Doña Mercedes and Pepito exhibit keen interest in hearing the reports.*] Some say that Don Julian discovered Teodora in my rooms, and that I attacked him in blind fury and killed him on the spot. Others—and these would seem to be my friends, since they raise me from the rank of vulgar assassin to the noble level of duellist—aver that we fought loyally like gentlemen. And there are others, again, who have the tale more accurately, and recount how Don Julian took my place in the arranged meeting with Nebreda—that I arrived late on the scene—either from design or fear, or because I was in the arms——but, no; it would burn my lips to give this version—the thought of it sets my brain on fire. Seek the basest, the vilest, that which most blackens—the filth of the mind, the mire of the soul, the dross of degraded consciences; cast it to the wind as it whistles along the streets upon bespattering tongues, and you will have the tale, and may see what reputation remains for an innocent woman and two honest men when the town takes to jabbering about them.

MERCEDES. It is sad, I admit; but perhaps public opinion is not altogether to blame.

PEPITO. Teodora did go to your rooms—she was there——

ERNEST. To prevent the duel with Nebreda.

PEPITO. Then why did she hide herself?

ERNEST. Because we feared her presence would be misconstrued.

PEPITO. The explanation is easy and simple. The difficult thing, Ernest, is to get us to believe it, for there is another still more easy and simple.

ERNEST. Which dishonours more, and that's the beauty of it.

PEPITO. Well, at least, admit that Teodora was giddy, if not really culpable.

ERNEST. Guilt is prudent and cautious. On the other hand, how imprudent is innocence!

PEPITO. Look here, if your rule holds good for everybody, the worst of us is an angel or a saint.

ERNEST. You are right. What does it matter? What is the weight or value of such calumny? The worst of it is that thought is degraded by mean contact with a mean idea. From force of dwelling upon a crime, the conscience becomes familiar with it. It shows itself terrible and repellent—*but it shows itself*—at night, in dark solitude! Yes—[*aside*] but what! why are they listening to me so strangely, almost in suspense? [*Aloud*] I am myself; my name is an honourable one. If I killed Nebreda solely because of a lie, what would I not do to myself if guilt threatened to give the truth to calumny?

PEPITO. [*Aside to Mercedes.*] He denied it! Why, it is as clear as daylight.

MERCEDES. [*Aside to Pepito.*]   He's wandering.

PEPITO. 'Tis only his confession he's making.

MERCEDES. [*Aloud.*]   That will do, Ernest.   Go, now.

ERNEST. Impossible, madam. I should go mad if I had to spend to-night away from this sick-room—out of my mind.

MERCEDES. But if Severo came and found you?

ERNEST. What do I care? He is a loyal gentleman. Better still, let him come. We fly from fear, and only the guilty are afraid. Nothing will make me run away, or acknowledge fear.

PEPITO. [*Listening.*]   Somebody is coming.

MERCEDES. Is it he?

PEPITO. [*Going down the stage.*]   No, 'tis Teodora.

ERNEST. Teodora! Teodora! I want to see her.

MERCEDES. [*Sternly.*]   Ernest!

ERNEST. Yes, I must ask her to forgive me.

MERCEDES. You don't remember——

ERNEST. I remember everything and understand. We two together! Ah, no. Enough. You need not fear. For her would I shed my blood, lay down my life, sacrifice my future, honour—all! But see her? never. 'Tis no longer possible. The mist of blood has risen between us. [*Goes out on the left.*]

SCENE V.

Doña Mercedes and Pepito.

MERCEDES. Leave me alone with her. Go inside to your father. I want to see into her heart, and shall be able to probe its depths with my tongue.

PEPITO. Then I will leave you together.

MERCEDES. Good-bye.

PEPITO. Good-bye. [*Goes out on the right.*]

MERCEDES. Now to put my plan into work.

SCENE VI

Teodora and Doña Mercedes. Teodora enters timidly, and stands near Don Julian's door on the right, listening anxiously, and muffling her sobs with her handkerchief.

MERCEDES. Teodora.

TEODORA. It is you. [*Advances to her.*]

MERCEDES. Courage! what good does crying do?

TEODORA. How is he? how is he? the truth!

MERCEDES. Much better.

TEODORA. Will he recover?

MERCEDES. I think so.

TEODORA. My God! My life for his.

MERCEDES. [*Draws her affectionately forward.*] And then —I have faith in your good sense. I can measure your remorse by your tears and anxiety.

TEODORA. Yes [*Doña Mercedes sits down with a satisfied air*], I did wrong, I know, in going to see him [*Doña Mercedes looks disappointed the confession is no worse*], but last night you told me about the outrage and the duel. I was grateful to you for doing so, although I did not then suspect the harm you did me, nor could I now explain it to you. Oh, what a night! [*Crosses her hands and glances upward.*] I have cried and raved, thinking of Julian's plight, of the scandal, of the violent quarrel and the bloodshed. Everything passed before my eyes—and then—poor Ernest dying, perhaps, for my sake! But why do you look at me so strangely? there can be no harm in it, surely! Or are you unconvinced, and do you think as the rest do?

MERCEDES. [*drily.*] I think your fear for that fellow's life altogether superfluous.

TEODORA. Why? with so skilled an antagonist! You have seen it—Julian——

MERCEDES. Julian has been avenged. The man who killed him no longer lives, so that you have been wasting your fears and your tears. [*With deliberate hardness.*]

TEODORA. [*Eagerly.*] It was Ernest——

MERCEDES. Yes, Ernest.

TEODORA. He met the viscount?

MERCEDES. Face to face.

TEODORA. [*Unable to restrain herself.*] How noble and brave!

MERCEDES. Teodora!

TEODORA. What do you mean? Tell me.

MERCEDES. [*Sternly.*] I can read your thought.

TEODORA. My thought!

MERCEDES. Yes.

TEODORA. Which?

MERCEDES. You know very well.

TEODORA. Have I no right to be glad because Julian is avenged? Is that an impulse I could be expected to repress?

MERCEDES. That was not your feeling.

TEODORA. You know so much more about it than I do!

MERCEDES. [*Pointedly.*] Believe me, admiration is not far from love.

TEODORA. What do I admire?

MERCEDES. This youth's courage.

TEODORA. His nobility.

MERCEDES. Quite so, but that's the beginning.

TEODORA. What folly!

MERCEDES. It *is* folly—but on your side.

TEODORA. You persist! Ever this accursed idea!—while it is with immense, with infinite pity that I am filled.

MERCEDES. For whom?

TEODORA. For whom else but Julian?

MERCEDES. Have you never learnt, Teodora, that in a woman's heart pity and forgetfulness may mean one and the same thing?

TEODORA. I beseech you—Mercedes—silence!

MERCEDES. I wish to let light in upon the state of your mind,—to turn upon it the lamp of truth, lit by my experience.

TEODORA. I hear you, but while I listen, it seems no longer a sister, a friend, a mother that speaks to me, so hateful are your words. Your lips seem to speak at inspiration of the devil's prompting. Why should you strive to convince me that little by little I am ceasing to love my husband, and that more and more I am imbued with an impure tenderness, with a feeling that burns and stains? I who love Julian as dearly as ever, who would give the last drop of blood in my body for a single breath of life for him—for him, from whom I am now separated—[*points to his room*]—why, I should like to go in there this moment, if your husband did not bar my way, and press Julian once more in my arms. I would so inundate him with my tears, and so close him round with the passion of my love, that its warmth would melt his doubts, and his soul would respond to the fervour of mine. But it is not because I adore my husband that I am bound to abhor the faithful and generous friend who so nobly risked his life for me. And if I don't hate him, is that a reason to conclude that I love him? The world can think such things. I hear such strange stories, and such sad events have happened, and calumny has so embittered me, that I find myself wondering if public opinion can be true,—in doubt of myself. Can it be that I really am the victim of a hideous passion, unconsciously influenced by it? and in some sad and weak moment shall I yield to the senses, and be subjugated by this tyrannous fire?

MERCEDES. You are speaking the truth?

TEODORA Can you doubt it?

MERCEDES. You really do not love him?

TEODORA. Mercedes, what words have I that will convince you? At another time, such a question would drive the blood of anger to my brow, and to-day, you see, I am discussing with you whether I am honest or not. Yes, am I really so? To the depth of the soul? No, for endurance of this humiliation proves me worthy of it. [*Hides her face in her hands and flings herself down in the arm-chair.*]

MERCEDES. Do not cry so, Teodora. I believe in you. Enough. No more tears. Let me but add one more word, and there's an end to the matter. Ernest is not what you believe him to be. He is not worthy of your trust.

TEODORA. He is good, Mercedes.

MERCEDES. No.

TEODORA. He is fond of Julian.

MERCEDES. He would betray him.

TEODORA. Again! My God!

MERCEDES. I no longer accuse you of responding to his passion, but I only assert—I would warn you that *he loves you.*

TEODORA. [*Rising in anger.*] Loves me!

MERCEDES. It is known to everybody. In this very room, a moment ago, before Pepito and me—you understand?

TEODORA. No, explain at once—what?

MERCEDES. He openly confessed it. He made a violent declaration, swore that he was ready to sacrifice life, honour, soul and conscience for you. And when you came, he wanted to see you. He only yielded to the force of my entreaties and went away. I tremble lest he should meet Severo and their encounter lead to an explosion. And you—what have you to say now?

TEODORA. [*Who has listened to Mercedes intently, held in an indefinable gloomy terror.*] Heavens above! Can it be true? and I who felt—who professed so sincere an affection for him!

MERCEDES. There, you are on the point of crying again.

TEODORA. The heart has no tears for the manifold deceptions of this miserable life. A lad so pure and finely natured,—and to see him now so debased and spotted! And you say that he actually uttered those words here—he!—Ernest. Oh, oh, Mercedes! send him away from this house.

MERCEDES. Ah, that is what I wanted. Your energy consoles me. [*With evidence of honest satisfaction.*] Pardon me—now I fully believe you. [*Embraces her.*]

TEODORA. And before? No? [*The actress must strongly accentuate this line.*]

MERCEDES. Hush! He is coming back.

TEODORA. [*Impetuously.*] I will not see him. Tell him so. Julian expects me. [*Goes to the right.*]

MERCEDES. [*Detaining her.*] Impossible! You must know it. He will not heed my orders, and now that I understand so fully how you feel for him, I should be glad to have him suffer at your hands the contempt he has already endured at mine.

TEODORA. Then leave me. [*Enter Ernest.*]

ERNEST. Teodora!

MERCEDES. [*Aside to Teodora.*] It is late, do your duty quickly. [*Aloud to Ernest.*] The command you heard a little while ago from me, you will receive again from Teodora's lips, and she is the mistress of this house.

TEODORA. [*In a low voice to Mercedes.*] Don't go away.

MERCEDES. [*To Teodora.*] Are you afraid?

TEODORA. I afraid! I am afraid of nothing. [*Makes a sign for her to go. Exit Doña Mercedes on the right.*]

SCENE VII

Teodora and Ernest.

ERNEST. The command was—that I should go away. [*Pause. Both remain silent without looking at each other.*] And you? Are you going to repeat it? [*Teodora nods, but still does not look at him.*] Have no fear, Teodora. I will respect and obey your order. [*Submissively.*] The others could not get me to obey them, little as they may like to hear it [*harshly*], but nothing you could say, even though you wound me—From you I will endure anything! [*Sadly.*]

TEODORA. I wound you! No, Ernest, you cannot believe

that—— [*Still does not look at him, is half vexed and afraid.*]

ERNEST. I do not believe it. [*Pause.*]

TEODORA. Adieu. I wish you all happiness.

ERNEST. Adieu, Teodora. [*Remains waiting for a moment to see if she will turn and offer him her hand. Then walks down the stage, turns back again, and approaches her. Teodora shows that she feels his movement, and is distressed, but continues to keep her face averted.*] If with my death at this very instant I could blot out all the misery that lies to my account, not through any fault of mine, but through an implacable fate, I should not now be standing here alive. You may believe it on the word of an honourable man. No shadow of the past would remain,—neither sighs nor pain to remember, nor that sorrowful pallor of your face [*Teodora starts and glances at him in terror*], nor the grieved fear of those eyes, nor sobs that tear the throat, nor tears that line the cheek. [*Teodora sobs.*]

TEODORA. [*Aside, moving further away.*] Mercedes was right, and I, blind and thoughtless that I was——

ERNEST. Bid me good-bye—once—for kindness's sake.

TEODORA. Good-bye! Yes; and I forgive you all the injury you have done us.

ERNEST. I, Teodora!

TEODORA. Yes, you.

ERNEST. What a look! What a tone!

TEODORA. No more, Ernest, I beseech you.

ERNEST. What have I done to deserve——?

TEODORA. It is all over between us. Regard me as one who no longer exists for you.

ERNEST. Is this contempt?

TEODORA. Go.

ERNEST. Go? in this way?

TEODORA. My husband is dying in there—and here I feel as if I too were dying. [*Staggers back and clutches the arm-chair to keep from falling.*]

ERNEST. Teodora. [*Rushes forward to support her.*]

TEODORA. [*Angrily drawing herself away.*] Don't touch me. [*Pause.*] Ah, I breathe again more freely. [*Tries to walk, staggers again weakly, and a second time Ernest offers to assist her. She repulses him.*]

ERNEST. Why not, Teodora?

TEODORA. Your touch would soil me.

ERNEST. I soil you!

TEODORA. Exactly.

ERNEST. I! [*Pause.*] What does she mean, Almighty God! She also! Oh, it is not possible! Oh, death is preferable to this—It cannot be true—I am raving—Say it is not true, Teodora—only one word—for justice—one word of pardon, of pity, of consolation, madam. I am resigned to go away, never to see you again, although 'twere to break, and mutilate, and destroy my life. But it will, at least, be bearable if I may carry into solitude your forgiveness, your affection, your esteem—only your pity, then. So that I still may think you believe me loyal and upright—that I could not, that I have not degraded you, much less be capable of insulting you. I care nothing about the world, and despise its affronts. Its passions inspire me with the profoundest disdain. Whether its mood be harsh or cruel, however it may talk of me and of what has happened, it will never think so ill of me as I do of it. But you, the purest dream of man's imagining—you for whom I would gladly give,—not only my life, but my right to heaven, ay, a thousand times—eagerly, joyously,—You, to suspect me of treason, of hypocrisy! Oh, this, Teodora—I cannot bear! [*Deeply moved, speaks despairingly.*]

TEODORA. [*With increasing nervousness.*] You have not understood me, Ernest. We must part.

ERNEST. But not like this!

TEODORA. Quickly, for mercy's sake. Julian suffers. [*Points to the sick-room.*]

ERNEST. I know it.

TEODORA. Then we should not forget it.

ERNEST. No; but I also suffer.

TEODORA. You, Ernest! why?

ERNEST. Through your contempt.

TEODORA. I feel none.

ERNEST. You have expressed it.

TEODORA. It was a lie.

ERNEST. No; not entirely. So that our sufferings are not equal. In this implacable strife *he* suffers as those on earth suffer, *I* as those in hell.

TEODORA. Spare me, Ernest—my head is on fire.

ERNEST. And my heart aches.

TEODORA. That will do, Ernest. I entreat you to pity me.

ERNEST. That was all I asked of you.

TEODORA. Mercy.

ERNEST. Yes, mercy. But why should you claim it? What is it you fear? of what are you thinking? [*Approaches her.*]

TEODORA. Forgive me if I have offended you.

ERNEST. Offended me, no! The truth, that is what I crave,—and I implore it on my knees. See, Teodora, my eyes are wet. [*Bends his knee before her and takes her hand. Don Julian's door opens, and Don Severo stands staring at them.*]

D. SEVERO. [*Aside.*] Miserable pair!

TEODORA. Don Severo!

SCENE VIII

Teodora, Ernest, and Don Severo. Ernest stands apart on the right. Don Severo places himself between him and Teodora.

D. SEVERO. [*In a low voice of concentrated anger, so that Don Julian may not hear.*] I can find no word or epithet adequate to the passion of contempt I would express, so I must be content to call you a blackguard. Leave this house at once.

ERNEST. [*Also in a low voice.*] My respect for Teodora, for this house, and for the sick man lying in yonder room, sir, compels me to put my retort—in silence.

D. SEVERO. [*Ironically, under the impression that Ernest is going.*] It's the best thing you can do—obey and hold your tongue.

ERNEST. You have not understood me. I do not intend to obey.

SEVERO. You remain?

ERNEST. Until Teodora commands me to go. I was on the point of going away for ever a moment ago, but the Almighty or the devil deterred me. Now you come and order me out, and as if your insult were an infernal message, it roots my heels to the floor in revolt.

SEVERO. We'll see that. There are servants to kick you out, and sticks if necessary.

ERNEST. Try it. [*Approaches Don Severo with a threatening air. Teodora rushes between them.*]

TEODORA. Ernest! [*Turns commandingly to Don Severo.*] You seem to forget that this is my house as long as my husband lives and is its owner. Only one of us two has the right to command here. [*Softens to Ernest.*] Not for him—but for my sake, because I am unhappy——

ERNEST. [*Unable to contain his joy at hearing himself defended by Teodora.*] You wish it, Teodora?

TEODORA. I beg it. [*Ernest bows and turns away.*]

SEVERO. Your audacity confounds and shocks me as much —no, far more, than his. [*Strides menacingly towards her. Ernest turns swiftly round, then makes a strong effort to control himself and moves away again.*] You dare to raise your head, wretched woman, and before me too! Shame on you! [*Ernest repeats previous movements and gestures, but this time more accentuated.*] You, so fearful and cowardly, where have you found courage to display this energy in his defence? How eloquent is passion! [*Ernest stands, looking back.*] But you forget that, before pitching him out, I had the authority to forbid the door of this house to you, who have stained its threshold with Julian's blood. Why have you returned? [*Seizes her brutally and drags her roughly toward himself.*]

ERNEST. No, I can't stand this—I cannot! [*He thrusts himself between Severo and Teodora.*] Off, you scoundrel.

SEVERO. Again!

ERNEST. Again.

SEVERO. You have dared to return?

ERNEST. You insolently affront Teodora. I still live.

What do you expect me to do, if not return and chastise you, and brand you as a coward?

SEVERO. Me?

ERNEST. Precisely.

TEODORA. No!

ERNEST. He has brought it on himself. I have seen him lift his hand in anger to you—you, you! So now—— [*Seizes Don Severo violently.*]

SEVERO. You impudent puppy!

ERNEST. True, but I'll not release you. You loved and respected your mother, I presume. For that reason you must respect Teodora, and humbly bow before a sorrow so immense as hers. This woman, sir, is purer, more honest than the mother of such a man as you.

SEVERO. This to me?

ERNEST. Yes, and I have not yet done.

SEVERO. Your life——

ERNEST. Oh, my life, as much as you like—but afterwards. [*Teodora endeavours to part them, but he pushes her gently away, without releasing Don Severo.*] You believe in a God—in a Maker—in hope. Well, then, as you bend your knee before the altar of that God above, so will I compel you to kneel to Teodora,—and that instantly, sir. Down—in the dust.

TEODORA. For mercy's sake——

ERNEST. To the ground! [*Forces Don Severo to kneel.*]

TEODORA. Enough, Ernest.

SEVERO. A thousand thunders.

ERNEST. At her feet!

SEVERO. You!

ERNEST. Yes, I.

SEVERO. For her?

ERNEST. For her.

TEODORA. That will do. Hush! [*She points in terror to Don Julian's door. Ernest releases Don Severo, who rises and moves backward. Teodora retreats and forms with Ernest a group in the background.*]

SCENE IX

Teodora, Ernest, Don Severo. Afterwards Don Julian and Doña Mercedes.

D. JULIAN. [*Inside.*] Let me go.

MERCEDES. [*Inside.*] No. You must not.

D. JULIAN. It is they. Don't you hear them?

TEODORA. [*To Ernest.*] Go.

SEVERO: [*To Ernest.*] Avenged!

ERNEST. I don't deny it. [*Enter Don Julian, pale and dying, leaning on Doña Mercedes' arm. Don Severo stations himself on the right, Ernest and Teodora remain in the background.*]

D. JULIAN. Together! Where are they going? Who detains them here? Away with you, traitors. [*Wants to rush at them, but strength fails him, and he staggers back:*]

SEVERO. [*Hurrying to his assistance.*] No, no.

D. JULIAN. Severo, they deceived me—they lied to me—the miserable pair! [*While he speaks Don Severo and Doña Mercedes lead him to the arm-chair.*] There, look at them—both—she and Ernest! Why are they together?

TEODORA AND ERNEST. [*Separating.*] No.

D. JULIAN. Why don't they come to me? Teodora!

TEODORA. [*Stretches out her arms but does not advance.*] Julian!

D. JULIAN. Here in my arms. [*Teodora runs forward and flings herself into Don Julian's arms, who clasps her feverishly. Pause.*] You see—you see—[*to Don Severo*] I know well enough they are deceiving me. I hold her thus in my arms. I crush and subdue her—I might kill her—so! and 'tis only what she deserves. But I look at her—*I look at her*—and then I cannot!

TEODORA. Julian——

D. JULIAN. [*Pointing to Ernest.*] And that fellow?

ERNEST. Sir!

D. JULIAN. I loved him! Silence, and come hither. [*Ernest approaches.*] You see, I am still her owner. [*He holds Teodora more tightly clasped.*]

TEODORA. Yes,—I am yours.

D. JULIAN. Drop pretence. Don't lie.

MERCEDES. [*Striving to soothe him.*] For pity's sake——

D. SEVERO. Julian!

D. JULIAN. [*To both.*] Peace. [*To Teodora.*] I see through you. I know well that you love him. [*Teodora and Ernest try to protest, but he will not let them.*] All Madrid knows it too—all Madrid.

ERNEST. No, father.

TEODORA. No.

D. JULIAN. They deny it—they deny it! Why, it is as clear as noonday. Why, I feel it in every fibre,—by the beat of fevered pulse, by the consuming flame of inward illumination!

ERNEST. It is the fever of your blood and the delirium of bodily weakness that feed the delusion. Listen to me, sir——

D. JULIAN. To hear how well you can lie?

ERNEST. [*Pointing to Teodora.*] She is innocent.

D. JULIAN. But I do not believe you.

ERNEST. Sir, by my father's memory——

D. JULIAN. Don't insult his name and memory.

ERNEST. By my mother's last kiss——

D. JULIAN. That kiss has long since been wiped from your brow.

ERNEST. What then do you want, father? I will swear by anything you wish. Oh, my father!

D. JULIAN. No oaths, or protests, or deceitful words.

ERNEST. Then what? Only tell me.

TEODORA. Yes, what, Julian?

D. JULIAN. Deeds.

ERNEST. What does he wish, Teodora? What does he ask of us?

TEODORA. I don't know. Oh, what are we to do, Ernest?

D. JULIAN. [*Watching them in feverish distrust.*] Ah, you would even deceive me to my face! You are plotting together, wretched traitors! I see it.

ERNEST. It is fever that misleads you—not the testimony of your eyes.

D. JULIAN. Fever, yes. And since fever is fire, it has

burnt away the bandage with which before you two had blinded me, and at last I see you for what you are. And now!—but why these glances at one another? Why, traitors? Why do your eyes gleam so? Tell me, Ernest. There are no tears in them to make them shine. Come nearer—nearer to me. [*Draws Ernest to him, bends his head, and then succeeds in thrusting him upon his knees. Thus Teodora is on one side of Don Julian and Ernest at his feet. Don Julian passes his hand across the young man's eyes.*] You see—no tears—they are quite dry.

ERNEST. Forgive me, forgive me!

D. JULIAN. You ask my forgiveness? Then you acknowledge your sin?

ERNEST. No.

D. JULIAN. Yes.

ERNEST. I say it is not so.

D. JULIAN. Then here before me, look at her.

D. SEVERO. Julian!

MERCEDES. Sir!

D. JULIAN. [*To Teodora and Ernest.*] Perhaps you are afraid? So it is not like a brother that you cherish her? If so, prove it. Let me see what sort of light shines in your eyes as they meet—whether, to my close inspection, the rays dart passion's flame, or mild affection. Come here, Teodora. Both—so—still nearer. [*Drags Teodora until she stumbles, so that both faces are compelled towards each other.*]

TEODORA. [*Frees herself with a violent effort.*] Oh, no.

ERNEST. [*Also strives to free himself, but is held in Don Julian's grasp.*] I cannot.

D. JULIAN. You love one another—you can't deny it, for I've seen it. [*To Ernest.*] Your life!

ERNEST. Yes.

D. JULIAN. Your blood!

ERNEST. All.

D. JULIAN. [*Forcing him to his knees.*] Stay still.

TEODORA. Julian!

D. JULIAN. Ah, you defend him, you defend him.

TEODORA. Not for his sake.

D. SEVERO. In God's name——

D. JULIAN. [*To Severo.*] Silence. [*Still holds Ernest down.*] Bad friend, bad son!

ERNEST. My father.

D. JULIAN. Disloyal! Traitor!

ERNEST. No, father.

D. JULIAN. Here is my shameful seal upon your cheek— To-day with my hand—soon with steel—so! [*With a supreme effort strikes Ernest. Ernest jumps up with a terrible cry, and turns away, covering his face.*]

ERNEST. Oh!

D. SEVERO. [*Stretches out his hand to Ernest.*] Justice.

TEODORA. My God! [*Hides her face in both hands, and drops on a chair.*]

MERCEDES. [*Turning to Ernest to exculpate Don Julian.*] It was only delirium.
   [*These four exclamations very hurried. A moment of stupor. Don Julian stands still staring at Ernest, and Doña Mercedes and Don Severo endeavour to calm him.*]

D. JULIAN. It was not delirium, it was chastisement, Heaven be praised. What did you think, ungrateful boy?

MERCEDES. That will do.

D. SEVERO. Come, Julian.

D. JULIAN. Yes, I am going. [*Is led away with difficulty between Don Severo and Doña Mercedes, and stops to look back at Teodora and Ernest.*]

MERCEDES. Quickly, Severo.

D. JULIAN. Look at them, the traitors! It was only justice—was it not? Say so—at least I believe it.

D. SEVERO. For God's sake, Julian—well, at any rate, for *mine*——

D. JULIAN. Yes, for yours, Severo, only for yours. You alone have loved me truly. [*Embraces him.*]

D. SEVERO. Yes, yes, it is so.

D. JULIAN. [*Stops at the door and looks back again.*] She is crying for him—and does not follow me. Not even a look. She does not see that I am dying—yes, dying.

D. SEVERO. Julian, Julian!

D. JULIAN. [*On the threshold.*] Wait, wait. Dishonour for dishonour. Good-bye, Ernest.
[*Exeunt Don Julian, Don Severo, and Mercedes.*]

SCENE X

Teodora and Ernest. Ernest drops into a chair near the table. Teodora remains standing on the right. Pause.

ERNEST. [*Aside.*] What is the use of loyalty?

TEODORA. And what is the use of innocence?

ERNEST. Conscience grows dark.

TEODORA. Pity, my God! Pity!

ERNEST. Pitiless destiny.

TEODORA. Oh, most miserable fate!

ERNEST. Poor child!

TEODORA. Poor Ernest! [*Both remain apart until now.*]

D. SEVERO. [*In anguish from within.*] My brother.

MERCEDES. Help!

PEPITO. Quickly. [*Ernest and Teodora move together.*]

TEODORA. They are crying.

ERNEST. He is dying.

TEODORA. Come at once.

ERNEST. Where?

TEODORA. To him.

ERNEST. We cannot. [*Detains her.*]

TEODORA. Why not? I want him to live.

ERNEST. And I!—but I cannot. [*Points to Don Julian's room.*]

TEODORA. Then I will. [*Rushes to the door.*]

LAST SCENE

Teodora, Ernest, Don Severo and Pepito. Ernest stands on the right in the middle of the stage, Teodora near the door of Don Julian's room. Pepito and, behind him, Don Severo, bar the way.

PEPITO. Where are you going?

TEODORA. [*In desperation.*] I must see him.

PEPITO. It is impossible.

D. SEVERO. She cannot pass. This woman must not

remain in my house—turn her out at once. [*To Pepito.*] No compassion—this very moment.

ERNEST. What!

TEODORA. My mind is wandering.

D. SEVERO. Though your mother should stand in front of that woman, Pepito, you have my orders. Obey them. Never mind her prayers or supplications. If she should cry—then let her cry. [*With concentrated fury.*] Away with her, away—else I might kill her.

TEODORA. Julian orders——

D. SEVERO. Yes, Julian.

ERNEST. Her husband! It cannot be.

TEODORA. I must see him.

D. SEVERO. Very well. Look at him, once more—and then—depart.

PEPITO. [*Interfering.*] Father——

D. SEVERO. [*Pushing him away.*] Stop, sir.

TEODORA. It can't be true.

PEPITO. This is too horrible.

TEODORA. It is a lie.

D. SEVERO. Come, Teodora—come and see. [*Seizes her arm and leads her to the door.*]

TEODORA. Oh! My husband! Julian—dead. [*Staggers shudderingly back, and falls half senseless.*]

ERNEST. [*Covering his face.*] My father! [*Pause. Don Severo watches them rancorously.*]

D. SEVERO. [*To his son.*] Turn her out.

ERNEST. [*Placing himself before Teodora.*] What cruelty!

PEPITO. [*Doubting.*] Sir——

SEVERO. [*To Pepito.*] Such are my orders. Do you doubt my word?

ERNEST. Pity.

D. SEVERO. [*Pointing to the death-chamber.*] Yes, such pity as she showed him.

ERNEST. Fire races through my veins. I will leave Spain, sir.

D. SEVERO. It makes no difference.

ERNEST. She will die.

D. SEVERO. Life is short.

ERNEST. For the last time——

D. SEVERO. No more. [*To his son.*] Ring.

ERNEST. But I tell you she is innocent. I swear it.

PEPITO. [*Interceding.*] Father——

D. SEVERO. [*With a contemptuous gesture.*] That fellow lies.

ERNEST. You impel me with the current. Then I will not struggle against it. I go with it. I cannot yet know what may be her opinion [*pointing to Teodora*] of others, and of your outrages. Her lips are silent, mute her thoughts. But what I think of it all—yes, I will tell you.

D. SEVERO. It is useless. It won't prevent me from—— [*Approaches Teodora.*]

PEPITO. [*Restraining him.*] Father——

ERNEST. Stay. [*Pause.*] Let nobody touch this woman. She is mine. The world has so desired it, and its decision I accept. It has driven her to my arms. Come, Teodora. [*He raises her, and sustains her.*] You cast her forth from here. We obey you.

D. SEVERO. At last, you blackguard!

ERNEST. Yes; now you are right. I will confess now. Do you want passion? Then passion and delirium. Do you want love? Then love—boundless love. Do you want more? Then more and more. Nothing daunts me. Yours the invention, I give it shelter. So you may tell the tale. It echoes through all this heroic town. But should any one ask you who was the infamous intermediary in this infamy, you will reply 'ourselves, without being aware of it, and with us the stupid chatter of busybodies.' Come, Teodora; my mother's spirit kisses your pure brow. Adieu, all. She belongs to me, and let heaven choose its day to judge between you and me. [*Gathers Teodora into his embrace, with a glance of defiance around.*]

CURTAIN

FINIS

FOLLY OR SAINTLINESS
A PLAY IN THREE ACTS

PERSONS OF THE DRAMA

DON LORENZO DE AVENDAÑA.

ÁNGELA, His Wife.

INÉS, Daughter of Both.

THE DUCHESS OF ALMONTE.

EDWARD, Her Son.

JUANA.

DR. TOMÁS.

DR. BERMÚDEZ.

BRAULIO.

BENITO.

SERVANT.

Scenes of the Play take place in the study of Don Lorenzo's house in Madrid.

ACT I

SCENE—*Don Lorenzo's study, octagon form. Fire lighting, over mantel-piece a large mirror in black frame L. Below, a door. Door and window R. Principal entrance in background. Book-shelves well filled R and L. Writing-desk and arm-chair L, sofa R. Scattered about in orderly confusion books and objects of art. Mounting severe and rich. A winter afternoon.*

SCENE I

DON LORENZO. [*Seated at table reading attentively.*] 'Mercy, my niece,' replied Don Quixote, 'is that which God this moment has shown me, despite my sins. Already my mind is clear and free, unclogged of the obscurities of ignorance, which my unhappy and incessant readings of those detestable books of chivalry cast upon me like a heavy shadow. Already have I sounded the depth of their delusions and absurdities, and I now regret nothing but that this awakening should have come so late that I have no longer time to seek compensation in reading those other books which are the light of the soul. I feel myself on the point of death, dear niece. I should like to depart in such a way that my life would not appear so evil as to obtain for me the reputation of madness; that, though it is true I have been mad, my death should not confirm its truth.' [*Stops reading, and remains a while in thought.*] Folly!

To struggle without truce or rest in this fierce battle of life for justice as Cervantes' immortal hero struggled in the world of his imagining! Folly! To love with an infinite love, and with the divine beauty of our desire ever beyond our reach, as was the Dulcinea he so passionately loved! Folly! To walk with the soul ever fronting the ideal, along the rough and prosaic path of human realities, which is like running after one of heaven's stars through crags and rocky places. Folly! Yes, so the doctors tell us; but of so inoffensive a form, and, upon the face of it, so little likely to prove contagious, that, to make an end of it, we do not need another Quixote. [*Pause. Rises and walks to the middle of the stage, where he stands thinking.*]

SCENE II

Don Lorenzo, Doña Ángela, and Dr. Tomás. The latter two stand at door on R., half-hidden by the curtains, and watch Don Lorenzo, whose back is toward them.

DOÑA ÁNGELA. Look at him! as usual, reading and thinking.

DR. TOMÁS. Madam, your husband is a sage, but wisdom may be overdone. For, if the tenser be the cord, the more piercing its notes, so the much easier is it to break. And when it breaks, to the divine note succeeds eternal silence. While the brain works in sublime spasms, madness is on the watch—don't forget it. [*Pause.*]

DON LORENZO. Strange book! Book of inspiration! How many problems Cervantes, unknowing perhaps, has propounded therein! The hero was mad, yes, mad [*pause*], he who only gave ear to the voice of duty upon the march of life; he who ceaselessly subjugated his passions, silenced his affections, and knew no other rule than justice, no other law than truth—and to truth and justice conformed each action: who, with a sacrilegious ambition, strove to attain the perfection of God above.

What a singular being he would appear in any human society! A new Quixote among so many Sanchos! Having to condemn the greed of this one, the vanity of that, the good fortune of this other, the uncontrolled appetites of another, and the frailties of all; in his own family, like the Knight Errant's housekeeper and niece; in his own friends not differing from the priest, the barber, and Samson Carrasco. And strong men and maidens, dukes and inn-keepers, Moors and Christians with one voice declaring him mad, until he himself should end by taking himself as such, or dying, feign to think so, that at least he might be left to die in peace.

DR. TOMÁS. [*Approaches Lorenzo, and places an arm on his shoulder. Doña Ángela also comes near.*] Lorenzo!

DON LORENZO. [*Turning round.*] Tomás!—Ángela!— you were here?

DR. TOMÁS. Yes; we were listening to part of your philosophical monologue. What has provoked these sublime self-revealings of my good friend?

DON LORENZO. I have been reading *Don Quixote*, and it has gone to my head, and there got mixed with the other tags of modern philosophy which are floating about, as my hard-hearted doctor would say, in the cells of grey substance.

DR. TOMÁS. So would anybody else say who wished to talk the language of reason.

DOÑA ÁNGELA. How dreadful! Are you two going to begin one of your interminable discussions on positivism, idealism, and all the other *isms* of the dictionary, which are so many abysses for common sense?

DR. TOMÁS. Don't be afraid, madam. I have something more interesting to say to Lorenzo.

DON LORENZO. [*To Dr. Tomás.*] And I have also something more urgent to ask you.

DOÑA ÁNGELA. I should think so indeed. Our child's health is surely more interesting and urgent than the follies and delusions with which your head is crammed.

DON LORENZO. [*Anxiously.*] How is my beloved girl to-day?

DOÑA ÁNGELA. Yes, how do you find Inés? [*Pause.*]

DON LORENZO. Do tell us. Don't keep us in suspense. [*Pause. Dr. Tomás shakes his head ominously*].

DOÑA ÁNGELA. For heaven's sake, doctor, tell me if there be any danger.

DON LORENZO. What are you saying, Ángela? Don't pronounce the word.

DR. TOMÁS. Softly, softly. You go too far. I don't, however, say that it is nothing serious.

DON LORENZO. What do you mean?

DOÑA ÁNGELA. Oh, what *do* you mean?

DON LORENZO. What is the matter with her? Has the illness a name?

DOÑA ÁNGELA. What are the remedies?—for I suppose it is curable. Oh, Dr. Tomás, you must indeed cure my child.

DR. TOMÁS. What is her malady? One of those that causes the greatest misfortune to mankind. What is its name? The poets call it love—we doctors give it another name. How is it cured? This very day, with the aid of the priest; and so excellent a specific is this, that after a month's appliance neither of the wedded pair retain a vestige of remembrance of the fatal sickness.

DOÑA ÁNGELA. What nonsense you do talk, Dr. Tomás! You had almost emptied my veins of their blood.

DR. TOMÁS. Well, to be serious. Given the condition of the young lady, her nervous temperament, her extreme susceptibility, and her romantic passion, the malady must be regarded as grave. And if you don't very speedily seek a remedy in the sweet security of marriage, my friend, I am grieved to say it, but duty compels me to inform you, that you need not count upon Inés. [*Gravely.*]

DON LORENZO. Tomás!

DOÑA ÁNGELA. You really believe——

DR. TOMÁS. I believe that Inés has inherited her father's excitable and fantastical imagination. To-day the fever of love runs like a fiery wave in her veins. If you don't marry her to Edward,—and that very soon—and she should be given to understand that her hopes are not destined to be realised, though I cannot predict in what way, I unhappily know that the delirium of fantasy, and the violence of her affection will eventually kill her.

DON LORENZO. Good God!

DOÑA ÁNGELA. My poor child!

DR. TOMÁS. You have my opinion, and I have given it in plain language as the urgency of the case demands, as well as my friendship for you, and our joint affection for the innocent child.

DOÑA ÁNGELA. [*To Don Lorenzo in a resolute tone.*] You have heard? We must marry Inés to Edward.

DON LORENZO. I would like it well indeed, Ángela. Edward is a good fellow, very intelligent, and passionately attached to our girl, but——

DOÑA ÁNGELA. But what? Are we not also noble, and why should Edward's mother, the Duchess of Almonte, oppose the union? And what matter if she does, since it is he, and not she, that is to be married?

Don Lorenzo. Ángela, think well upon it. Ought we to encourage a son in revolt against his mother?

Doña Ángela. *You* think well upon it. Lorenzo, ought we to sacrifice our child to that woman's vanity?

Don Lorenzo. It is easy enough to lament vanity and misfortune. The important thing is to find a remedy against evil.

Doña Ángela. Why not speak to the duchess? They say she is a kind woman, apart from her aristocratic pretensions, and that she idolises Edward. Let us go to her, and beseech and implore her.

Don Lorenzo. I beseech! I implore! Humiliate myself! It is certainly not my place to entreat for her son's hand. She it is who should come to my house and beg for that of my daughter. Social convention, the respect of woman, and my own honour ordain it so.

Doña Ángela. Here you see the philosopher, the sage, the perfect man overflowing with vanity and pride. [*Goes over to Dr. Tomás who is standing at table reading.*]

Don Lorenzo. You are unjust, Ángela. It is not pride, but common dignity—yes, dignity. It is not honourable to us to go a-begging on Inés' behalf the ducal coronet another family chooses to withhold from her—she who wears herself a far fairer crown. I repeat, it would not be to our credit to go from door to door, still less to emblazoned doors, with hands held out for the alms of a name, when Inés bears my name, as good, as untarnished and honourable as any other, however great it may be.

Dr. Tomás. Lorenzo is right—you, too, madam, are right.

Doña Ángela. Never mind, you need not go. Preserve intact your dignity of sage and philosopher. I who am only a poor mother will go. It will not hurt me to go from door to door a-begging, not coronets, nor coats of arms, but the life and happiness of my child.

DON LORENZO. Nor will it me, Ángela. You it is who are right. Let the world say what it will. Let the duchess think what she will, I will go. [*To Dr. Tomás.*] It is my duty, is it not? Your judgment is upright and austere, and you can pronounce dispassionately. Give me your frank opinion.

DOÑA ÁNGELA. Ah, what a man! Now don't stay to discuss whether or no you ought to go. These things, my lord philosopher and husband, are decided by the heart, and not by the head. It is something to be thankful for that you have not gone back to your books to seek solution of the problem. It is a wonder you are not hunting among the German metaphysicians, or the Greek classics, or in that unintelligible tangle of mathematics, to see if any author by chance has treated of the future marriage of Miss Inés de Avendaña with Edward de Almeida, Duke of Almonte, proving the insuperable difficulties by *a* plus *b*, and for the sake of *a* plus *b* you would meanwhile let my poor child die.

DON LORENZO. Don't turn me into ridicule, Angela. You know I adore Inés.

SCENE III

Don Lorenzo, Ángela, Dr. Tomás, and Inés. Inés enters by door on R. as Don Lorenzo utters these words, and stands still on hearing her own name.

DON LORENZO. For her life! For her happiness! Why, to dry one tear of her eyes would I give all those my own could shed. For one bright hour for my Inés would I gladly turn all the remaining hours of my life into martyrdom. [*Inés, without being seen by the rest, holds out her arms to her father lovingly, and kisses her hand to him.*] There, say no more upon the subject. This very day will I go and see the duchess. I will implore, supplicate, humiliate myself if necessary, and she must yield. She won't? [*Joyous movement of Inés. Doña Ángela effusively takes her husband's hand.*] Well, if I have not got titles, I have at least a name, which, though I may not be able to make it illustrious by work and study——

DR. TOMÁS. It is illustrious, my dear fellow.

DON LORENZO. Illustrious, no—but respectable, yes. Besides, I have some millions that I have inherited, and which I will make over to the duchess and to Edward, that they may be enabled thereby to renovate a coronet somewhat the worse for wear. So you may be sure of it. Inés will be happy, and her happiness will be ours.

DOÑA ÁNGELA. And yours—also ours, who live in you— you, my husband, who are, when science does not blunt your sense, the best, the kindest, and most loving of men.

INÉS. Oh, heavens! [*Gives signs of faintness, and leans against door.*]

DOÑA ÁNGELA. [*Rushes over to her.*] Inés, my child.

DON LORENZO. Inés, Inés! What's the matter?

DR. TOMÁS. [*Approaching.*] Come, girl, what nonsense is this?

INÉS. [*Sits down on sofa R., the rest stand around her.*] Nothing. It's nothing—it is only—I feel I would like to laugh, and tears instantly rise to my eyes—and then I want to cry, and I feel so glad, so happy that I cannot. It is because I am fond, very fond of you, father. [*Embraces him affectionately.*] How kind you are, and how good God has made you! I am happy, very happy. [*Throws herself sobbingly into her mother's arms.*]

DOÑA ANGELA. That's it, my girl, weep. It will do you good. See how kind your father is. You must love him dearly.

INÉS. With all my heart. When are you going? To-day? Is it not so?

DR. TOMÁS. [*Laughing at her fond assurances.*] Ah, selfish girl! We are very fond of papa when he does something to please us? But if he did not go to the duchess's, should we be quite so fond of him—quite!—as now?

INÉS. Just the same.

DR. TOMÁS. [*Doubtingly.*] Quite the same?

INÉS. [*Maliciously.*] It is possible I should be so sad that I might not think of saying it.

DR. TOMÁS. I thought so.

INÉS. Before, I felt something weigh upon my breast, and choke me. Now, without any effort—thus—spontaneously—as delicious tears of happiness flow—endearing words break from me. Before, I was only able to say: 'unhappy I, father!' Now, I don't think of myself, I think of him, and my heart rises to my lips upon a cry of love—'how dear you are to me!' [*Again embraces her father.*]

DON LORENZO. Inés, my daughter!

INÉS. And you also, mother, you also. [*Embraces Doña Angela. Don Lorenzo and Dr. Tomás move away from sofa, where Doña Angela and Ines remain seated, and come to the middle of the stage.*]

DR. TOMÁS. Poor philosopher! Neither of those two has read a single page of all your books, and both know more than you do. You think yourself strong, and in their hands you are as soft as wax. You think yourself a sage, and in their arms you are an innocent, not to say a fool. You think yourself just and uncorruptible, and upon the will of those two women you could be led into any injustice or weakness.

DON LORENZO. No, Tomás. When I am sustained by principle my will is iron.

DR. TOMÁS. I don't say 'we shall see,' because they are both angels—but, alas! if they were other! Permit me to parody the great poet, and exclaim with him: 'Temptation, thy name is woman!'

DON LORENZO. [*Energetically.*] 'Words, words, words,' he said before that, doubtless, in prescience of the parody.

DR. TOMÁS. There you are, up on the rostrum already.

INÉS. Don't tease papa.

DON LORENZO. The doctor's sallies don't annoy me, child.

DR. TOMÁS. This is where we stand—that for affection, for friendship, for love, for what you call the mysterious attraction of one soul for another, we can and should arrive at——

DON LORENZO. Even sacrifice—yes. But never do wrong.

DR. TOMÁS. A pretty maxim for a book on morality.

DON LORENZO. A still better one for the conscience.

DR. TOMÁS. And are there no cases in which, to prevent greater misfortunes, one may compromise with this Cato's conscience, for just a little, a very little fault, hardly as big as a grain of sand?

DON LORENZO. Once accepted, your grain would quickly weigh as heavily as a mountain of granite.

DR. TOMÁS. Now, you are up the mountains. The rostrum does not suffice.

INÉS. That will do, Dr. Tomás. You mustn't say such things to papa.

DR. TOMÁS. Let us sum up the matter. It is war to the knife against all evil under any form or disguise whatsoever. Not so?

DON LORENZO. So it is.

DR. TOMÁS. Then let us instantly apply your theory. But truly I had forgotten it, and it is quite a romance. Lend me your attention. Listen, ladies. [*Doña Angela and Inés approach.*]

DON LORENZO. What is it?

DR. TOMÁS. To-day a woman begged me to take you in her name——

DON LORENZO. What?

DR. TOMÁS. A kiss.

DOÑA ÁNGELA. To him?

DON LORENZO. To me?

DR. TOMÁS. Yes. [*To Doña Ángela.*] But don't be alarmed, dear madam. It is the kiss of an aged dame, and it comes drenched in tears. 'Tis but the last and dolorous contraction of dying lips,—the final adieu of a being who, in a few brief hours, will have breathed her last.

DON LORENZO. I cannot imagine——

DR. TOMÁS. She—this poor woman—sent for me this morning. I mounted to the garret where she lies dying. She named herself, otherwise I should never have recognised her. She swore she was innocent, and all the same begged me to intercede with you for her pardon.

DON LORENZO. You are talking a language not one word of which do I understand.

DR. TOMÁS. Do you remember your mother's death?

Don Lorenzo. What a question! I never knew my father. He died when I was an infant. But my mother! Ah, poor mother! [*With emotion.*]

Dr. Tomás. Do you remember how, suddenly feeling herself in the throes of death, she wanted to speak to you and could not; and then in a kind of convulsion seized the locket she always wore round her neck and put it into your hands, fixing you with the supreme anguish of her gaze already dimmed with the eternal shadow?

Don Lorenzo. Yes, I remember. Continue.

Dr. Tomás. Finally, you remember that upon your mother's death you lost consciousness, when the locket disappeared. You have not forgotten who was accused of the robbery?

Don Lorenzo. She! It is she? my poor nurse, Juana!

Dr. Tomás. Yes, it is indeed that same Juana who is dying a few yards off in a miserable garret—Juana who implores your pardon in the sad kiss she sends you.

Don Lorenzo. Juana, my second mother, who for twenty-five years was a real mother to me. But why do you speak of pardon? What compromise can there be here with wrong? Forgiveness is no compromise, nor does the poor old creature need my forgiveness. She capable—impossible!

Dr. Tomás. Not so impossible. When the maid who had care of your mother's jewels notified the loss of the magnificent locket in diamonds to the police, and the first investigation was made, Juana denied having it, and yet it was subsequently discovered that she had taken it from you when you fainted. Two days afterwards she was surprised concealing it behind a porcelain vase. She was arrested, you remember, condemned, and suffered imprisonment for the robbery, and only through your influence and strong recommendation, recovered, if not her lost honour, at least her liberty.

Don Lorenzo. [*Firing.*] All the same, I persist in saying that Juana accused, Juana on the bench of infamy, Juana in shameful seclusion, was innocent, and that human justice erred.

Dr. Tomás. Appearances——

Don Lorenzo. Not infrequently deceive.

Dr. Tomás. Then how do you explain it?

Don Lorenzo. There must be an explanation. There is some mystery which we do not understand.

Dr. Tomás. [*To Doña Ángela.*] Now he is off on the hunt of mysteries—in a search for a supernatural explanation of an act that to my mind finds a very natural and simple explanation in human frailty.

Don Lorenzo. But I know that my poor nurse was incapable of an action so base. I would have defended her if the illness that prostrated me after my mother's death had not prevented me. And as soon as I obtained her freedom, the poor woman disappeared, which fact caused me many a bitter tear. God knows how unweariedly I sought her everywhere. God knows how I longed for her return to me—and she!—how cruel of her! Why did she not come back? No, Juana, my good friend, you must not die until I have clasped you once more in my arms, until I have given you back your farewell kiss. [*With increasing agitation touches a bell and servant in livery appears.*] Say—a carriage—at once—instantly—I am going to bring her back here—this very moment. Do you not feel that it is my duty, Ángela—and you, too, Inés?

Doña Ángela. In any case it is a work of charity.

Don Lorenzo. It is a just reparation. [*Exit by door L.*]

Dr. Tomás. He is the best of men, and the most credulous. He will believe, as an article of faith, anything that the poor old creature may tell him. He will even help her to invent some extravagant tale. Ah, madam, we ought to make an examination of this library like that great and witty one the priest and barber made of the ingenious hidalgo's library.

DOÑA ÁNGELA. Oh, if I only could.
   [*Enter Don Lorenzo in out-door dress on L.*]

DON LORENZO. Well, I'm off. You will come too, to help me to bring her back. [*To Dr. Tomás.*]

DR. TOMÁS. I am yours to command.

DON LORENZO. Do you think it safe to move her?

DR. TOMÁS. The unfortunate woman is sinking rapidly. She is just as likely to die in her garret as on the cushions of your carriage, or crossing the threshold of this, to her, enchanted palace. It is, however, quite possible that joy may revive her, and lend her another few hours of existence.

DON LORENZO. Then come along. Good-bye, Ángela; good-bye, Inés.

INÉS. Good-bye. [*Caressingly.*] And afterwards you will go to see the duchess, won't you?

DON LORENZO. Yes, child, afterwards. You can wait, but not so that poor woman. She comes first, Inés.

DOÑA ÁNGELA. [*Apart to Dr. Tomás.*] Can you assure me that my daughter runs no risks if we marry her?

DR. TOMÁS. Only those of marriage, madam, which are none of the slightest.
   [*Exeunt Doña Ángela and Dr. Tomás by door C. talking together. Behind them, Don Lorenzo takes leave of Inés at the door.*]

SCENE IV

Inés claps her hand joyously like a child as she returns to the middle of the stage.

INÉS. He will speak this very day to the duchess. He has promised, and he may be relied upon, for he never breaks his word. That is settled, then. He will see her, and my father speaks so well! Why, is he not a man of vast learning? He is certain to convince her. If such a man as he were not able to persuade the duchess that Edward and I ought to be married, of what avail his having studied so much? Why possess so many books in French, in Italian, in German, and even in Greek? Such futile learning! But no, he will twist her round his finger. Besides, they all say that she is a saint. How could she be anything else, being Edward's mother? A saint, do they say? But if, being such, she refused to allow Edward to marry me, what sort of sanctity would her's be? and of what its use? What nonsense! of course we shall be married—why, we must, and it is I who say it. [*Pause.*] It seems impossible—like a dream. Good gracious, if it should prove a dream, then let me never awake. But it is no dream. This is my father's study. Those are his books. [*Approaches the bookcase.*] Newton, Kant, Hegel, Humboldt, Shakespeare, Lagrange, Plato, St. Thomas—It is very certain that if it were a dream I should not remember all those names, for what do I know of such illustrious gentlemen? [*Looks over balcony.*] I can be sure that it is no dream, for there is rain falling, falling. What a delightful thing rain is! The air seems converted into little bars of crystal. And in yonder mirror I can see myself. [*Goes over to looking-glass with coquettish play.*] It is certainly myself whom I know so well. I, with my oval face, which Edward finds so perfect. Fancy his taste! with my hazel eyes, which Edward finds so lovely. Was there ever such another as he for telling pretty lies? But truly at this moment, what with delight and the heat of the fire, my eyes do shine with an extraordinary brightness. I should like to be pretty—prettier than ever—for his sake, for his dear sake. But why does he not come? It is very late. Now that I want so much to see him, he won't come. You see he won't come—men are so selfish and horrid.

SCENE V

Inés and Edward.

INÉS. [*Going toward him.*] Edward, Edward!

EDWARD. My darling.

INÉS. How late you are!

EDWARD. [*Submissively.*] I always come at two o'clock.

INÉS. It is now three.

EDWARD. Is it possible? [*Looks at his watch.*] No, my beloved, it is only a quarter to two.

INÉS. [*Authoritatively.*] It is three o'clock.

EDWARD. [*Shows her his watch.*] A quarter to two. Are you convinced? [*Points to the clock on mantelpiece.*] And look there—it is the same hour.

INÉS. [*Offended.*] Well, I suppose you are right. What an accomplished lover to haggle over minutes! It is always too early to come, too late to stay with his Inés, and he subjects the beats of his heart to the measurements of his time-piece.

EDWARD. [*Beseechingly.*] Inés.

INÉS. Go away, go away. It is not yet two—it still wants fifteen minutes to the hour. Go and take a turn about the streets, and look at the people, and come back at two sharp.

EDWARD. Inés!

INÉS. That is your hour for coming. A nice thing indeed if you were to come earlier. What would the Astronomical Observatory think of that?

EDWARD. Do forgive me—I was wrong.

INÉS. No, the error was mine. Desire hastens onward the hours for me, and you, to punish me, come and hold up a watch before my eyes. [*Makes a quick movement and seems to hold something to his face.*] What a poetic lover!

EDWARD. I confess my fault. I repent and humbly beg your pardon.

INÉS. Ah, you admit it. That is better.

EDWARD. You see I was so happy and delighted to come that I quite lost knowledge of what I was saying, and even now I scarcely know what it is I am saying.

INÉS. It was also wrong of me to scold you so, Edward. But I was so gay, so wild with eagerness in my desire to see you, that the moments seemed centuries to me.

EDWARD. Ah, I have to tell you, my own——

INÉS. [*Pays no heed to him.*] I have such great news for you.

EDWARD. [*Also does not heed her.*] At last we are within reach of bliss.

INÉS. I should think so—for life.

EDWARD. How improbable it looks!

INÉS. My father has promised this day—this very day—you understand?—But you are not listening.

EDWARD. [*Still not heeding her.*] My mother——

INÉS. Your mother! What?

EDWARD. She is coming here in half an hour to propose our marriage.

INÉS. The duchess!

EDWARD. [*With comic gravity.*] Her grace, the Duchess of Almonte, will have the honour to beg this white hand [*takes her hand*] of Mr. and Mrs. Avendaña for her son Edward, although that same Edward has long since possessed himself of it, and holds it warm against his heart, and I have small faith in his being persuaded to relinquish it, even should it be refused him.

INÉS. She! really—she is coming! Ah, every one was right to call that woman a saint.

EDWARD. That woman is my mother. She loves me with all her heart, and this morning I besought her with tears in my eyes, and she, with answering tears, flung her arms round me and yielded to my prayer. She attaches first importance to the glorious deeds of her ancestors, and worships honour fanatically, and would far sooner see me dead than my name linked with one that bore the slightest stain. But she fully appreciates the worth of Don Lorenzo, his scientific renown—which is another kind of glory—and his——

INÉS. That will do. We have enough of the tale—the conclusion is that she comes here to-day, that we are to be married, and that we are going to be immeasurably happy—is it not so? That is the chief thing—at least it is so for me—I cannot answer for you.

EDWARD. Ungrateful girl! Do you doubt me?

INÉS. I do not doubt you. But how lucky it is for me that your mother has consented!——if not! You love me dearly, I know—but you——a mother has a claim upon your obedience. If she said 'No,' like a good son, Edward—not so?—you would have spared her pain, and despite your soul's deep sorrow, you would have left your poor Inés, who so tenderly loves you. Don't listen, bad boy! Let nobody hear the whisper—but, indeed, I do love you so much that without you—see how foolish I am!—I should have died of grief.

EDWARD. Dearest!

INÉS. So you see how grateful I ought to be to your mother, since it is not to you but to her that I owe my happiness.

EDWARD. You cruel girl! Don't you know what I should have done in spite of every obstacle? You feel it.

INÉS. Yes. You would have obeyed and given me up.

EDWARD. Never,—for nothing, for nobody.

INÉS. Will you swear it?

EDWARD. I swear it by all that is holy.

INÉS. There, I am content.

EDWARD. And I most blissful.

SCENE VI

Inés, Edward, Juana, Don Lorenzo, and Dr. Tomás. Juana appears in door C. supported by Don Lorenzo and Dr. Tomás, stands for breath and then slowly advances; is poorly and darkly clad.

EDWARD. [*Turning round.*] What a sombre group! Why does this black cloud come to dim the azure of our heaven?

INÉS. It is Juana, my father's nurse. Oh, it is quite a story. I will tell it to you afterwards.

DON LORENZO. Easy, Juana, easy——

JUANA. Who is that young lady?

DON LORENZO. Inés, my daughter. Come hither, Inés. [*Inés approaches, followed by Edward.*]

JUANA. How very lovely! She looks like an angel. To find such a creature at one's side in the hour of eternal darkness would seem a presage of heaven.

Don Lorenzo. Another step.

Dr. Tomás. One more effort—the last. [*They help her to the sofa, where she sits down. The rest stand round her.*]

Juana. I should like to kiss her. [*Points to Inés, who comes nearer. Juana takes her hand and draws her to her.*] No, your hand is warm and my breath is ice. I may not kiss you! It would be to give you the kiss of death. [*Pushes her gently away and lets her hand fall.*] Not with the lips, but in thought do I kiss you.

Dr. Tomás. [*To Edward and Inés.*] Come away. The poor woman wants to be alone with him. [*To Juana.*] Till later, and courage. Your pains are over.

Juana. Yes, those of this world.

Inés. Poor woman! [*Stands and looks at her.*]

Edward. Come, my darling.
[*Exeunt Dr Tomás, Inés, and Edward, R.*]

SCENE VII

Don Lorenzo and Juana.

Juana. [*After a pause.*] Have they already gone?

Don Lorenzo. Yes, dear Juana. We are alone.

Juana. At last. At last has come the hour so long desired. All things come—and all things pass! Listen to me, Lorenzo. Life is slipping from me so quickly, so quickly, and I have still so many things to say to you. The first is—I am innocent. I did not think—I did not want—I did——[*Tears interrupt her.*]

Don Lorenzo. I know it, Juana—I know it.

Juana. You do not know. Everything is against me—everything.

Don Lorenzo. I beg you not to worry yourself in this way. Forget all, and rest.

JUANA. Forget, yes. I shall soon enough forget. Rest! I have so much time before me for resting that to-day I desire to live—although I suffer, although I weep. I would carry with me into the grave even the tears and sobs along with the kisses—that its silence and solitude might be filled with some remembrance of life. [*Pause.*] That is why I want to tell you something. But how can I without preparing you? Now, so that doubt may not come first before revelation, and before doubt suspicion, and before suspicion presentiment, and before presentiment that nameless something, the shadow cast upon the soul by that which comes from afar? You do not understand me, and I do not know how to explain myself, though it is now twenty years since I first harboured the one idea. Judge if I ought to be able to explain it well.

DON LORENZO. Tell me anything you like, only do not get excited over it.

JUANA. Yes, I will tell you all. How could I die without doing so? In the first place, if only to prove to you that I am not a miserable—thief. [*Hides her face.*]

DON LORENZO. Hush, hush! Do not pronounce the word.

JUANA. And then—the sole consolation left me is to open my heart to you. Forgive me, Lorenzo. The dying are so selfish. For you it will be a horrible shock—while for me it will be a supreme benediction.

DON LORENZO. If it were so for you, my dear Juana, how could it be a horrible shock for me?

JUANA. How! But so it will be—so it will be, my son. My son! Give me leave to name you such. You are not angry with me?—truly?

DON LORENZO. I beseech you, Juana!

JUANA. Well, then, my son will I call you, and you too

must call me mother. Call me mother, once. Let it please heaven or hell, mother you must name me.

DON LORENZO. Mother!

JUANA. Not so—not in that way. Cruel boy! [*Leans to embrace him. Jerks herself back and falls on sofa.*]

DON LORENZO. Poor woman! She is delirious.

SCENE VIII

Juana, Don Lorenzo, and Inés. Inés rushes in C. in high spirits and approaches her father. She is excited and can hardly speak.

INÉS. Father, father—the duchess—is coming. She is coming here—can't you guess?

DON LORENZO. The duchess!

INÉS. Yes—to speak to you about—Edward has persuaded——

DON LORENZO. What good news, my dearest girl! At last God wills——

INÉS. You are pleased?

DON LORENZO. [*Caresses her.*] And you?

INÉS. Yes, if you are also. Come, come quickly.

JUANA. [*Seizes Don Lorenzo's arm.*] No, I cannot let you go. Don't leave me.

DON LORENZO. [*To Inés.*] I will be with you presently.

INÉS. Don't delay—oh, be sure and not delay, If you offend her——

DON LORENZO. You need not fear. Let Ángela receive her in the drawing-room with all ceremony. I will carry Juana up to her room, and join you in a moment.
[*Exit Inés C.*]

SCENE IX

DON LORENZO. [*Tries to lift Juana and she resists.*] Come, Juana, come and rest. Afterwards we will talk as much as you like.

JUANA. Afterwards, no. Suppose I should die before!

DON LORENZO. [*Impatiently.*] Nonsense; you mustn't think of such a thing.

JUANA. It is twenty years since I have seen you, and now they won't leave us together an instant. It is very cruel of them.

DON LORENZO. [*Again tries to raise her.*] Afterwards, my good Juana.

JUANA. And you too want to leave me—you too! Ah, I can compel you to stay with me.

DON LORENZO. Juana!

JUANA. Listen—one word, and then you are free, if you still wish to leave me. It was I, I myself, who stole the locket.

DON LORENZO. You!

JUANA. Yes.

DON LORENZO. What for?

JUANA. So that you might not see it.

DON LORENZO. Why?

JUANA. Because there was a paper in it containing something your mother had written that I did not want you to see.

DON LORENZO. What was it?

JUANA. I know the words by heart. They were:

'Lorenzo, my son, in the casket which lies at the head of my bed there is hidden a paper under a sealed envelope. When I am dead, open it, and read what I wrote during a night of sharp remorse. Forgive me, and may God inspire you.'

DON LORENZO. [*In surprise.*] 'Forgive me, and may God inspire you.' She wrote that?

JUANA. Yes.

DON LORENZO. You also made strange mention of remorse. [*With increasing curiosity.*]

JUANA. Remorse was the word. Now go away if you like.

DON LORENZO. [*Thinking.*] No. [*Pause.*] And that paper?

JUANA. It was no secret for me that your mother had written it. Where it was hidden was what I did not know. That there was something hidden in the locket a vigilance so alert as mine had easily discovered, and what the paper contained misgiving helped me to divine. That was why I took the locket. It was mine by right. It had cost me twenty years of tears and anguish, than which none more bitter or intolerable have ever been shed.

DON LORENZO. Forgiveness, remorse, a secret—and my mother! I cannot imagine what you would say. Confused shades gather and drift before my mind, and pain strikes my heart in lightning flashes. You are raving, and you make me rave too.

JUANA. No, no.

DON LORENZO. But that secret paper in the casket——

JUANA. It was mine, and you did not see it because it was not right you should see it. Since your mother was dead, what could it matter to her? Have I not said it, —there is nothing more selfish than death?

DON LORENZO. That paper——

JUANA. I have it.

DON LORENZO. Here?

JUANA. Here. [*Lifts her hand to her bosom.*] Look, it is but a sheet of paper, and yet it weighs so heavily upon my heart.

DON LORENZO. I must see it.

SCENE X

Juana, Don Lorenzo, Dr. Tomás behind.

DR. TOMÁS. Lorenzo, Lorenzo!

DON LORENZO. [*Impatiently.*] What do you want?

DR. TOMÁS. The duchess has come.

DON LORENZO. An appropriate hour.

DR. TOMÁS. [*Aside.*] What a tone! [*Aloud.*] Come and receive her.

DON LORENZO. Yes, I'll go.

JUANA. Don't leave me, for Christ's sake. By all that is most sacred to you I implore you to stay. [*Aside.*] If he only knew.

DR. TOMÁS. Are you coming?

DON LORENZO. Yes,—yes; but don't worry me. I've told you before, I'll go.

JUANA. Do not leave me. I will tell you everything, everything. I will give you that paper—which your mother wrote twenty years ago—her letter—her signature—you will see. But only don't leave me yet.

DR. TOMÁS. [*Angrily.*] Come, Lorenzo.

DON LORENZO. I said I would go—but afterwards. I know when I ought to go. Now leave us. [*To Juana.*] Give me the paper.

JUANA. As soon as that man goes away.

DON LORENZO. [*Violently.*] Will you go!

DR. TOMÁS. But the duchess——

DON LORENZO. Let her wait. Has she never kept others waiting in her ante-chambers? Well, then, mine are at least as good as hers.

DR. TOMÁS. Are you out of your senses?

DON LORENZO. I am in them well enough, but not in yours, where I should be ill at ease. Leave me at once.

DR. TOMÁS. What can be the matter, Lorenzo? [*Approaches him eagerly.*]

DON LORENZO. Nothing, nothing. I am tired of hearing you. For heaven's sake leave me alone.

DR. TOMÁS. Very well, very well. But what the deuce has come over the man?

SCENE XI

Don Lorenzo and Juana.

DON LORENZO. Now we are alone.

JUANA. Lorenzo!

DON LORENZO. What is it? Do you distrust me? Then I will go away. Promise to give me that paper. My child's happiness awaits me yonder, and nevertheless a hand of iron, the hand of implacable fate retains me here by your side. Consider, Juana, if I am resolved to probe this secret.

JUANA. Lorenzo!

DON LORENZO. The paper! Since it was written by my mother, it is mine.

JUANA. Don't be angry with me, Lorenzo, dear one. It is here. [*Takes it from her bosom.*] This is it.

DON LORENZO. [*Tries to seize it.*] Give it me.

JUANA. Wait, wait. I will read it myself. I will read it more slowly than you—and thus you will be spared a too sudden knowledge of the truth.

DON LORENZO. Then read on, and let us see.

JUANA. Yes, dear, but do not look at me. Only listen. [*Holds the paper so that Don Lorenzo shall not see the contents; reads.*] 'Lorenzo, my son, forgive me——'

DON LORENZO. Again!

JUANA. [*Reading.*] 'I feel that the end of life is near for me, and remorse has taken hold of me.' [*Pause.*]

DON LORENZO. Continue.

JUANA. 'I wish to tell you the truth, and I love you too greatly to do so. Read the secret of your existence in these lines stained by my tears, and do then as you will.'

DON LORENZO. The secret of my existence! Give it me. [*Tries to snatch the paper from her.*]

JUANA. No.

DON LORENZO. What nightmare is this, Juana? You seem to have encircled my head with a band of iron that presses intolerably across my temples. Give me that paper.

JUANA. No. God help me!

DON LORENZO. You must. [*Seizes the paper, and reads with intense emotion.*] 'Your father was rich, very rich. He possessed millions. I was very poor. We had no children——' We had no children, she says——

SCENE XII

Don Lorenzo, Juana, Doña Ángela. Afterwards Edward.

DOÑA ÁNGELA. [*Enters precipitately.*] The duchess!

DON LORENZO. [*Angrily, while Juana tears paper from him, and conceals it.*] Again! leave me alone. What do you want?

DOÑA ÁNGELA. Lorenzo, Lorenzo.

EDWARD. [*Rushes in.*] Don Lorenzo!

DON LORENZO. You, also—go away, go all of you.

DOÑA ÁNGELA. Mercy upon us, what is this? What can it mean? What is the matter with you, Lorenzo? do be sensible.

DON LORENZO. Away, away! I implore, if needs be I am ready to kneel to you, but only leave me. Oh, human selfishness! They think there is nothing else besides their passions and interests. Tomás, Ángela, Edward, the duchess—all of them. Ah, it is the dropping of water on the skull.

EDWARD. But, sir, my mother is coming——

DOÑA ÁNGELA. Yes, the duchess, tired of waiting, is coming.

EDWARD. She says she is coming herself to seek the sage in his den.

DON LORENZO. Then let her come. But leave me, leave me all of you, if you would not drive me wild.

DOÑA ÁNGELA. [*To Edward.*] It is impossible for your mother to see him in this state.

EDWARD. Come, madam, we will go and keep her in the

gallery to gain time. Perhaps Inés will be able to
soothe him in a little while.

[*Exeunt Edward and Doña Ángela.*]

SCENE XIII

Don Lorenzo and Juana.

DON LORENZO. The paper! that accursed paper! Where is it? You have it.

JUANA. [*Showing it.*] Yes.

DON LORENZO. Then give it me. 'We had no children,' she said. [*Makes an unsuccessful effort to read.*] Where is it? I don't know. The letters swim before me. My eyes are dim. 'We had no children!' I cannot read, I can't. Do me the kindness to read it for me. [*Juana takes the paper.*] Ah, there, where it says: 'We had no children.'

JUANA. [*Reads.*] 'My husband knew that an incurable disease was rapidly undermining his health. Death went with him, nestled in his heart. Mad with love for me, he wished to secure me all his fortune, and I—it was wrong, I know now, it was wrong, for he had a father living, but I,—oh, forgive me, Lorenzo, you who are so kind and honourable—I accepted.' [*Pause.*]

DON LORENZO. Continue, continue.

JUANA. 'We looked about for a child. I cannot write any more. Juana knows the secret. She will tell you all. Once more, I implore you to forgive me. Farewell, Lorenzo, and may God counsel you. I loved you like a son, though you were no child of ours.'

DON LORENZO. I—I—was not—what does it mean? Not her son? I bear a name that is not mine! For forty years have I enjoyed a fortune that belonged to others. I have robbed everything—social position, name and wealth. All, all! Even my mother's caresses, since she was not my mother,—even her kisses, since I was not her son. No, no. This is not possible. I am not so base. Juana, Juana, for the love you bear the God above, tell me the truth. Look, it is not for my own sake—what does it matter what happens to me?—but for my family's sake—for those unfortunate women—for my dear child's sake, my beloved Inés, who will die of it, and you see, I cannot let her die. [*Bursts into desperate sobs.*]

JUANA. That is true. But hush! Who need know of it? and then it will not matter.

DON LORENZO. But if it be true?

JUANA. [*In a low voice.*] It is true.

DON LORENZO. It seems a lie. That woman who cherished me so tenderly was not my mother?

JUANA. No. Your mother loved you still more.

DON LORENZO. Who was she, then?

JUANA. Lorenzo!

DON LORENZO. What was her name?

JUANA. Look at me without anger, and I will tell you.

DON LORENZO. Where is she?

JUANA. In strife with the torments of hell.

DON LORENZO. Is she also dead?

JUANA. She is dying. [*Towards the end of this dialogue Juana raises herself, and both stand in nervous agitation, staring wildly. When she utters the last word, she falls back again powerless upon the sofa.*]

DON LORENZO. Juana!

JUANA. [*Contorted with pain.*] Not that name!

DON LORENZO. Mother!

JUANA. Yes, call me so—my son! [*Makes a supreme effort to hold him to her.*]

SCENE XIV

Don Lorenzo, Juana, and Dr. Tomás.

DR. TOMÁS. Here she is—she is coming.

JUANA. [*Freeing herself.*] Leave me—they are coming, and I do not wish them to see me.

DON LORENZO. No—wait—I scarce know what I would say to you, but I have much to tell you.

JUANA. Afterwards—Good-bye now, I can die content. I have called him son. [*Exit slowly R. Don Lorenzo follows her, and Dr. Tomás stands watching them.*]

DON LORENZO. No, not yet. [*Juana disappears behind curtain. Don Lorenzo would follow, but is detained by Dr. Tomás, and obliged to return to the middle of the stage.*]

SCENE XV

Don Lorenzo, Ángela, Inés, the Duchess, Edward, and Dr. Tomás.

DUCHESS. [*With exquisite courtesy.*] Señor de Avendaña.

DON LORENZO. Avendaña, Avendaña! I don't know where he is, madam. [*In sombre absent tone.*]

DOÑA ÁNGELA. [*Aside.*] What is he saying?

INÉS. Goodness, what does this mean?

DUCHESS. I understand, Señor de Avendaña, how unwelcome must be my visit, since I come to claim of you the most precious of your possessions [*points to Inés*], and certainly it is not surprising that you should receive me as an enemy. [*Sweetly.*]

DON LORENZO. Fate is my enemy, nobody else, madam.

INÉS. [*Aside.*] Oh, what can have happened?

DUCHESS. You are right. It is the ruthless enemy of the parents.

DON LORENZO. Still more so of the children.

DUCHESS. I do not deny it. But in spite of it, 'tis divine law that governs our human sorrows, and we are forced to respect it. [*Makes an effort to turn the conversation, but does not conceal her wonderment.*]

DON LORENZO. Ah, madam, those laws might often prove less cruel if it were only human cruelty that dictated them. [*The duchess evinces marked impatience. Edward approaches her. Inés goes to her father, while Doña Angela and Dr. Tomás look on gloomily.*]

INÉS. [*Aside to Don Lorenzo.*] Father, I entreat you——

EDWARD. [*Aside to Duchess.*] For my sake, mother.

DUCHESS. [*Haughtily and dryly.*] I am a mother, and I adore my son. I know that happiness is not possible for him without this young lady, and rather than lose one child I prefer to gain two.

INÉS. [*To Don Lorenzo.*] See how kind she is, father.

DON LORENZO. To lose a son were a terrible misfortune.

DUCHESS. [*Gently and approaching Don Lorenzo.*] Will you not consent to bestow also the name of son upon my boy?

INÉS. [*In low voice of entreaty.*] Answer, father.

DON LORENZO. [*Looks sadly at his daughter, takes her*

head between his hands, and contemplates her yearningly.] How sweet you are! It seems incredible that you should not prove stronger than the law of honour.

DUCHESS. [*Unable to control herself.*] To make an end of the matter, Señor de Avendaña, do you wish my son, the Duke of Almonte, to give his name to your daughter Inés?

DON LORENZO. [*In magnificent fury.*] If I were a scoundrel, madam, this were an excellent occasion for procuring an honest name for my nameless child.

INÉS. Father!

DR. TOMÁS.
DOÑA ÁNGELA. } Lorenzo!

DUCHESS. I must frankly confess that I can make nothing of your answers nor of your attitude, which is quite other than what I had expected. I will content myself with asking for the last time—do you consent?

DON LORENZO. I am an honourable man. Misfortune may conquer me, but it will never disgrace me. Your Grace, this marriage is impossible.

DUCHESS. [*Offended, retreats a step.*] Ah!

INÉS. What do you say, father? Impossible!

DON LORENZO. Yes, impossible. For I am not Avendaña. My parents were not my parents. This house is not my house. To you, my dearest girl, I can only give a soiled and an unworthy name,—because I am the wretchedest of men and I do not wish to be the basest.

INÉS. Father, father—oh, why are you killing me? [*Falls into a chair.*]

DOÑA ÁNGELA. What have you done, you madman?

DON LORENZO. Inés, my child! Thou hast conquered, O God; but have pity on me.

ACT II

SCENE—*The same as First Act. Night, a fire is burning, a shaded candle on the study table.*

SCENE I

Edward listens at door R., then comes up C.

EDWARD. I hear nothing. Has she recovered consciousness? To think how close a thing to life is death! [*Pause.*] They believe that I must give up my beloved girl! They suppose me capable of crediting Don Lorenzo's absurd tale. Poor scholar! Why, he doesn't know what he is saying. [*Pause.*] And even if his assertion were true, would that make Inés other than the loveliest, the most adorable of women? Mine she will be, though I should have to cast myself at my mother's feet and bathe them with my tears. Don Lorenzo must consent, even if we have to gag him and put him into a strait-jacket. And that wretched beggar from whom the ill-advised philosopher has caught his delirium must be sent away, far away from everybody. How will my poor Inés bear up against the blow her father has inflicted upon her? [*Again approaches the door and listens.*] Nothing, nothing. Silence, always the same silence. [*Comes down.*] Her father! her own father! Heaven help me, but I almost hate the man. [*With increasing passion.*] The madman! How he delighted to torture her! Her father!—that brainless scholar! an atheist clothed in sanctity! a new Don Quixote *minus* wit and *plus* pedantry! a mock Bayard of honour! What sort of father is he who pretends to a reputation for virtue through his daughter's broken heart? A fig for such virtue! Vice itself is more lovable. No one comes, and the hours go by—ah, I hear somebody coming at last.

SCENE II

Edward and the Duchess, who enters R.

EDWARD. How is Inés, mother? Has she regained consciousness?

DUCHESS. She has now, thank God. Poor child! I could not go until I was assured it was all right, and that she was better. And you, my son?

EDWARD. I must see her.

DUCHESS. Edward!

EDWARD. Then we have to talk to Don Lorenzo, and afterwards——

DUCHESS. Afterwards you will get to the end of my patience. I have done all for you that honour, dignity, and social convention permit—even more. But the moment has come for you to show yourself a man, to remember who you are and listen to the voice of duty.

EDWARD. Rightly said, mother, that is what I am prepared to do, but it remains to be seen if we entertain the same idea of duty.

DUCHESS. You must give Inés up.

EDWARD. Why? Because of her poverty?

DUCHESS. By no means.

EDWARD. Then why, mother? Because Don Lorenzo

wishes to perform a sublime action which, if he carries out the prospect, will immortalise him in tale and history, and, who knows, may even lift him aloft into the Calendar?

DUCHESS. I see you appreciate the humour of the situation, and that is no bad sign.

EDWARD. I want to show you how perfectly cool I am. As for Don Lorenzo, we must regard the affair as a joke, or put him into an asylum.

DUCHESS. Don't say such things, Edward. It offends me to hear you speak so. There may be some slight exaggeration, perhaps no inconsiderable precipitation, and a certain air of melodramatic display in Don Lorenzo's project, but we cannot deny that he is acting like a gentleman.

EDWARD. Why does he revel in his daughter's misfortune?

DUCHESS. Because he is accomplishing his duty without respect of human passions.

EDWARD. Then if Don Lorenzo is so honourable, and the lustre of noble actions is a heritage, Inés will be something more than the angel of my life—she will bring me a wealth of hereditary virtue.

DUCHESS. She will also bring more than her share of hereditary dishonour. [*In low voice approaching him.*] The girl has no name good or bad, since nobody knows what her father's is, and that of her grandmother has been inscribed as a thief's upon the infamous register of a prison.

EDWARD. Hush!

DUCHESS. If we are to believe Don Lorenzo, that unhappy girl's fate is to be a humble nurse's grandchild, and her father's accomplice in living under a false name. It would perhaps be an excess of aristocratic pride to reject such an honourable alliance, but to such a decision am I led by what you, with your modern education, will doubtless qualify as old-fashioned prejudices.

EDWARD. Well, mother, I love Inés.

DUCHESS. You are mad, boy.

EDWARD. That were not strange, since love is said to be a madness.

DUCHESS. You almost make me lose my judgment.

EDWARD. Would you prefer to lose me?

DUCHESS. Enough, Edward. We must leave this house which, in an evil moment, I entered to-day for the first time.

EDWARD. But say—is not Inés sweet?

DUCHESS. Assuredly—as an angel of God's heaven, when I first beheld her, and now she looks like the angel of sorrow.

EDWARD. Does not the whole world regard Don Lorenzo as an accomplished scholar, and have you yourself not said that he is a saint?

DUCHESS. It would be injustice to deny the value of a reputation so illustrious as his, or the keenness of his sense of honour.

EDWARD. Then there is no objection to him.

DUCHESS. Certainly not.

EDWARD. [*Approaches the duchess and speaks in a low voice.*] Can't we find some means of averting scandal? Who knows anything of this wretched story, true or false, though to me it seems more likely false? Only ourselves, and we will hold our tongue. Dr. Tomás is almost one of the family. Death will shortly seal the lips of that unhappy woman. And, after all, Don Lorenzo is a father; he will do for Inés' sake that which you refuse to do for mine. Why, mother dear, need we go in search of misery and death when felicity is within our reach?

DUCHESS. Ah, see how contact with crime perverts the noblest minds! Unfortunate boy, do you not understand that you are proposing a monstrous thing to me? that you wish me to be an accomplice to a felony? Good heavens, what has come over you that you should think and speak such things?

EDWARD. Who on earth speaks of anything monstrous or proposes felony? Have we all gone mad with Don Lorenzo, or are you martyrising me for your own entertainment?

DUCHESS. You suggested our averting scandal by silence.

EDWARD. Yes.

DUCHESS. Then——

EDWARD. Listen, mother. This is what I meant to say. If Don Lorenzo's tale be true, which is what I doubt, the legitimate heirs of this confounded wealth may be discovered cautiously, in secret, and a way can be found to restore it to them.

DUCHESS. But on what pretext?

EDWARD. If you had to beg for a fortune, it might be difficult to find one, but when it comes to giving, don't be afraid. It is easy enough, and any pretext is equally welcome to those who receive it.

DUCHESS. Inés will still bear a name she has no title to.

EDWARD. She will bear mine, which is worth all others.

DUCHESS. That is true. But Don Lorenzo——

EDWARD. Leave him alone. He has enough to do with his philosophy. We have ourselves to think of, and I believe that it can be all managed if you will consent.

With a word you can give Inés back life, and give a new life to me in exchange for that which your unkindness blighted, and which I first owed to your affection. Restore happiness to this unhappy family, and bestow their usurped fortune upon the rightful heirs without noise or vain display. This is no felony, and it is not a monstrous thing to do.

DUCHESS. You magnetise me, Edward. I scarce know what to say. But an inward voice warns me that what you suggest is neither right nor just,—that deception can never be preferable to truth, and despite Don Lorenzo's ravings, I feel that duty triumphs in him, while in you it is passion that triumphs, for all your arguments.

EDWARD. How so? Tell me.

DUCHESS. I cannot discuss it with you, Edward.

EDWARD. What you cannot do is love me as you ought.

DUCHESS. Not love you; cruel boy! You have wounded me to the heart, though I know that you do not believe what you say.

EDWARD. Then yield to me.

DUCHESS. Don't press me, Edward.

EDWARD. You are yielding—I see it. Your face is pale, there are tears in your eyes, and your lips tremble. [*Caressingly.*] Confession of consent hangs upon them —yes, why not? What is there absolutely opposed to that high ideal of honour you and Don Lorenzo worship? What wrong is there in my plan?

DUCHESS. There is wrong, Edward.

EDWARD. So little, an atom, a shadow, a mere scruple. And don't I deserve you should commit so trivial an error for me? Go among the people whom you treat with such contempt, and from whom the aristocrat's pride separates you by an abyss; seek out a mother, and ask her if, for her son's sake, she would not stifle upon a cry of love all these refinements of conscience.

DUCHESS. [*Passionately.*] I am capable of making any sacrifice a mother can make.

EDWARD. [*Embracing her.*] Thanks, mother, thanks.

DUCHESS. But——

EDWARD. You have promised, you have promised. [*Without heeding her.*] And, after all, it may not even be necessary. What assurance have we that Don Lorenzo's tale is true? What tangible proofs are there? None that we know of. The word of a dying woman in delirium? Is that enough?

DUCHESS. Truly not.

EDWARD. Yet we have not even that much; for Dr. Tomás has not been able to interrogate Juana. How do we know that she told it to Don Lorenzo, or if he only dreamed it? Let me assure you, Don Lorenzo's head is no sound one.

DUCHESS. It is not, indeed.

EDWARD. What an odd and extravagant fellow he is!

DUCHESS. For my part, I really thought he had gone mad.

EDWARD. Depend upon it, he is not far off. All these men of learning end that way. Both Dr. Tomás and Ángela admit that he doesn't reason like other men.

SCENE III

The Duchess, Edward, and Doña Ángela.

DOÑA ÁNGELA. For pity's sake, madam, do not leave us yet. Inés wishes to see you. She calls upon your name through heart-breaking sobs, for you are her sole consolation.

DUCHESS. Poor child!

DOÑA ÁNGELA. She will not remain in bed, though we begged her to do so, and her nervous agitation is such that she fills us with terror. If strength had not failed her, she would have come to look for you. In kindness, duchess, do go to my stricken girl, and console her, you who are so affectionate a mother. 'Tis a most afflicted mother that implores you.

EDWARD. And you will tell her that there is still hope, that all depends upon Don Lorenzo—won't you?

DOÑA ÁNGELA. What? Is it true? Oh, madam—— [*To duchess, and takes her hand effusively.*]

EDWARD. Yes [*to Doña Ángela*], I will explain it. You must persuade your husband.

DUCHESS. But—— [*Edward does not heed her, and talks aside to Doña Ángela.*] That boy of mine does just what he likes with me. What am I to say to this good woman now that he has promised my consent? Oh, what a hare-brained fellow! The girl herself is lovely, like a dream, and altogether very charming. Poor Inés!—and Don Lorenzo possesses, or rather did possess, a colossal fortune. Ah! what things are human might and human vanity!

DOÑA ÁNGELA. [*To Edward.*] I understand, I understand. [*Then comes over to the duchess.*] I am very grateful to you for your great kindness. Do, pray, carry the good news yourself to my daughter, and I, in a little while, will induce Lorenzo to consent. Never fear, he will give in. It is certain, else will he prove himself quite heartless.

EDWARD. Come, mother.

DUCHESS. What am I to do?

EDWARD. How good of you!
[*Exeunt Duchess and Edward, R.*]

SCENE IV

Doña Ángela, Don Lorenzo, enters door L.

DON LORENZO. My mother dying—and yonder that other morsel of my soul! What can I do, my God? [*Walks slowly toward door R. and meets Doña Ángela.*]

DOÑA ÁNGELA. Where are you going, Lorenzo?

DON LORENZO. To see my daughter.

DOÑA ÁNGELA. Impossible. She has recovered consciousness now, and your presence might again upset her, since you it was who caused her illness.

DON LORENZO. But I wish to see her.

DOÑA ÁNGELA. You cannot. With you duty is always imperative, so you will respect that unhappy girl's grieving solitude [*ironically*], not upon the command of my will, which must always be second to yours, but upon that of your own reflective judgment.

DON LORENZO. You are right. [*Pause. Both are in middle of stage.*] My own beloved daughter! What does she say of me?

DOÑA ÁNGELA. Nothing.

DON LORENZO. She does not blame me?

DOÑA ÁNGELA. I cannot answer for the murmurings of sorrow in her heart.

DON LORENZO. I to be her executioner! to destroy all her hopes! Can it be that I have broken her heart?

DOÑA ÁNGELA. You know full well what you have done, Lorenzo. So much the better, if remorse will now help you to repair your cruel work.

Don Lorenzo. I am indeed miserable.

Doña Ángela. You miserable! Inés it is who is miserable, not you, who doubtless find assured ineffable joy and divine consolation in contemplating your own moral perfection. [*Ironically.*]

Don Lorenzo. How ill you judge me, and how little you understand me!

Doña Ángela. I judge you ill, and yet humbly admire the fruit of your sainthood! That I do not understand you, I admit, for superior beings such as you are not within reach of so mediocre an intelligence as mine.

Don Lorenzo. Ángela, your words pierce my heart like a sharp dagger.

Doña Ángela. Your heart! impossible.

Don Lorenzo. But what would you have me do? Speak, advise, decide—bring light to a mind that gropes among shadows.

Doña Ángela. What would I have you do? Whatever you like now. Only save your child. Place no fresh obstacle to this marriage. Don't continue to irritate the duchess's pride by brutal and futile revelations. Don't make it impossible for us to remedy the evil you have done by any new explosion.

Don Lorenzo. Frankly, then, you would have me hold my tongue.

Doña Ángela. That is it. Hold your tongue.

Don Lorenzo. But that would be infamous.

Doña Ángela. I know nothing about it. I feel, I can't argue.

Don Lorenzo. My whole soul rises up in revolt against the idea. To become an accomplice in the most repugnant, because most cowardly, of crimes! To enjoy usurped wealth and a name I have no right to, and all that is not ours! God has not willed it so, and what he has not willed should not be. Inés, you and I, all sunk in the mire! Is this what you would counsel? [*With increasing excitement.*] Then virtue is but a lie, and you all, whom I have most loved in this world, perceiving what I regarded as divinity in you, are only miserable egoists, incapable of sacrifice, a prey to greed and the mere playthings of passion. Then you are all but clay, and nothing more. And if you are but clay, resolve yourselves to dust, and let the wind of the tempest carry all off. [*Violently.*]

DOÑA ÁNGELA. Lorenzo!

DON LORENZO. Beings shaped without conscience or free will are simply atoms that meet to-day and separate to-morrow. Such is matter—then let it go.

DOÑA ÁNGELA. You are wandering, Lorenzo. I don't understand you. I don't know what it is you want.

DON LORENZO. To respect truth and justice.

DOÑA ÁNGELA. Truth!

DON LORENZO. Yes.

DOÑA ÁNGELA. And cry it to the world from the house-tops.

DON LORENZO. I will announce it.

DOÑA ÁNGELA. And leave us in poverty.

DON LORENZO. I will earn your bread and my own by my work.

DOÑA ÁNGELA. You earn your bread! Scholar's vanity! Well, be it so, but listen to me first. If it should be that we really have no right to our wealth, give it up,—well and good. [*Don Lorenzo bursts into a cry of delight and advances to her with outstretched arms.*] Privations do not fright me, nor am I the miserable woman and egoist you painted erewhile.

DON LORENZO. Ángela, my dear wife, forgive me.

DOÑA ÁNGELA. Do you want my forgiveness? Do you want me to continue blessing the hour I became your wife, as I have always blessed it till to-day?

DON LORENZO. Yes.

DOÑA ÁNGELA. Then do your duty as a man of honour, but in silence, prudently, without ostentation, or noise, or scandal.

DON LORENZO. Why? The duchess would never consent to her son's marriage with Inés even at that price.

DOÑA ÁNGELA. Edward answers for his mother's consent.

DON LORENZO. She will never give in.

DOÑA ÁNGELA. She will. She is a woman and a mother. We have not all attained such perfection as yours.

DON LORENZO. I do not believe it.

DOÑA ÁNGELA. Is it that you do not believe it, or that you fear it?

DON LORENZO. But supposing she should consent,—how can I retain a name that is not mine?

DOÑA ÁNGELA. What shabby subtleties to sacrifice my Inés to!

DON LORENZO. A name, Ángela, in social life is——

DOÑA ÁNGELA. A name is but a sound, a passing breath of air, something vain and evanescent. But a child, Lorenzo, is a creature made of our own flesh and of the blood in our veins: a creature that, while still nothing, we shelter warm in our bosom, and receive into our arms upon its first cry; that gives us its first smile and its first kiss; that lives by our life, and is at once our sweetest joy and our sharpest sorrow: a creature we love more than ourselves, but without a taste of that selfish leaven which degrades all our other loves; the sole divine affection that exists upon this earth, and if heaven be heaven, beyond the blue it will also be found in God himself. Choose now between what you call a name, and what I call a child.

DON LORENZO. Your words madden me.

DOÑA ÁNGELA. If you first lost your senses for Inés' misfortune, it matters little that I should drive you mad for her good.

DON LORENZO. You are partly right, Ángela. I am a poor fool. My scruples are, perhaps, exaggerated. My daughter, my dear Inés—she, so good, so lovely—she would die,—would surely die.

DOÑA ÁNGELA. At last, Lorenzo, my dear husband.

DON LORENZO. But stay—no—my ideas are confused. My brain turns to the flail of a fiery whirlwind. Yet I still feel convinced that it would not be enough to renounce my fortune. I am bound to say why I renounce it.

DOÑA ÁNGELA. Lorenzo!

DON LORENZO. [*Not listening to her, but talking to himself.*] It is true that without it I could always materially make restitution of material possessions,—and still without recognising the legitimate rights of those I have despoiled. 'Twould be to make a traitorous and cowardly restitution, under shadow of vain and artificial rights, which I must fabricate for my convenience, and for the benefit of my family, instead of openly and honourably relinquishing what is not mine.

DOÑA ÁNGELA. What nonsense you talk, Lorenzo!

DON LORENZO. [*Not heeding her.*] If I retain a name that is not mine, I prove myself a shabby thief—I am compelled to pronounce a word that burns on my lips. I rob a name and all its rights, and I deprive my victims of their best means of defence against a cupidity that may any day develop in my descendants, and perhaps give rise to a worse iniquity in the future. Don't you see it? Surely you must see it if you are not totally blind! I must tell the truth, the whole truth, in a loud voice, happen what will.

DOÑA ÁNGELA. Lorenzo!

DON LORENZO. Would a judge and a tribunal sentence me to despoilment of my goods alone, or to despoilment of both my goods and my name? Of everything, everything—is it not so? Then what a judge would decide I have to do myself—my own judge—or I am a wretched fellow. Such, my poor wife, is what my conscience ordains me to do. I want no half-hearted view of honesty, for there is no middle term between clean honour and complete abasement. All this is quite clear to me. Nothing so clear as duty.

DOÑA ÁNGELA. Very well, if the affair is made public the duchess will not give her consent.

DON LORENZO. She will not consent. 'Tis what I have already said.

DOÑA ÁNGELA. Ah, Lorenzo, Lorenzo, you are everything,—philosopher, moralist, jurisconsult, and, needless to say, gentleman. All, all, wretched reflecting machine, except a father.

DON LORENZO. If you want to drive me out of my senses you are succeeding.

DOÑA ÁNGELA. That would indeed be difficult.

DON LORENZO. Because I am out of them already?

DOÑA ÁNGELA. Yes, but you haven't yet got to the bottom of the abyss. Hear me, Lorenzo, for I, too, understand something of logic—after all, am I not your wife? It is your intention to tell the truth, the entire truth?

Don Lorenzo. It is so.

Doña Ángela. Before the tribunal of human justice?

Don Lorenzo. We need not trouble ourselves about divine justice, which at this moment is weighing you and me.

Doña Ángela. Understand me well, Lorenzo. I want to know if you will repeat to the judge, to the lawyers and all, no matter whom, whose business it will be to take possession of your abandoned fortune in the interests of the rightful owners, the story you told us a little while ago?

Don Lorenzo. Yes.

Doña Ángela. You will tell them everything?

Don Lorenzo. I am bound to do so.

Doña Ángela. Hear me further. You will have to acknowledge Juana the nurse as your mother.

Don Lorenzo. That is the only way left me to wipe away the stain of an iniquitous sentence. Here alone were reason sufficient to prove the crime of the silence you counsel.

Doña Ángela. And here, I say, is reason sufficient to command silence as an imperative duty. Can't you see that if Juana be innocent of the wrong imputed, she is guilty of a much greater,—which is called illegal retention of personal rights? You know it well. Falsification of a family is quite as bad as degrading or destroying it. To deprive legitimate owners of their fortune is far worse than to lift a locket from the ground. To conceal an illegitimate birth under an honest name is the same as covering the plague-spot of vice with an ermine mantle. If Juana be your mother, all this has she done, and has persisted in the deception for forty years.

Don Lorenzo. [*Moves away and grasps his head in both hands.*] Silence, for God Almighty's sake, silence!

Doña Ángela. That is just what I am begging of you—silence!

Don Lorenzo. She is my mother.

Doña Ángela. What of that? He who can injure an innocent daughter need not trouble himself to respect a culpable mother. Is not divine law above human law? Is not justice first?—Justice, duty, and truth? Must not the command of the spirit ever triumph over the weaknesses of the flesh?

Don Lorenzo. You speak well—but in spite of it you are raving. [*Moves away from her.*]

Doña Ángela. And why? You seem already to be growing as ordinary and weak as any poor mother. Does duty not order you to let your daughter die? Then let her die. Does it not also command you to cast the dying Juana into a prison-cell? Then hasten to procure her condemnation. You see, Lorenzo, I have some logic too, in my own way.

Don Lorenzo. Infernal logic.

Doña Ángela. And yours? From what sublime sphere does it descend?

Don Lorenzo. [*Moves still further off.*] Let me be, let me be. I can stand no more. My own Inés—and my mother! What have I done to you, Ángela, that you should torture me so? [*Falls nervously into arm-chair at table.*] My head burns; it is on fire.

Doña Ángela. [*Gently.*] Lorenzo, Lorenzo.

Don Lorenzo. Yes, you are right, and I am a poor fool. How can I know what I ought to do? Darkness envelops me. What is truth? What is falsehood?

Doña Ángela. [*Aside.*] It was very cruel of me, but I

149

have saved my child. He will not speak. [*Don Lorenzo seated, sinks down in chair, with his arms upon table, and hides his face in both hands. Doña Ángela approaches him caressingly and speaks tenderly.*] Forgive me, Lorenzo.

DON LORENZO. Go away—in mercy leave me.

DOÑA ÁNGELA. I wanted to show you the abyss you were falling into. I wanted to save Inés, and to save you yourself from your own outbreak.

DON LORENZO. Yes, yes, Ángela. I understand, but leave me now.

DOÑA ÁNGELA. Do you forgive me?

DON LORENZO. I forgive you—and love you. Poor Ángela, you too are suffering. But I desire to be alone.

DOÑA ÁNGELA. Very well. I am going. But do not fret. We shall find some way out of the difficulty. I will tell Inés that you want to see her—you would like to speak to her and comfort her?

DON LORENZO. [*Submissively.*] If she wishes it.

DOÑA ÁNGELA. Then wait here, and I will come for you presently, and then, beside our child, together, at one in our desire and with a common will, you'll see that we shall get the better of fatality which now seems to crush us.

DON LORENZO. We'll conquer it, yes, we'll conquer it. [*Speaks unconsciously.*]

DOÑA ÁNGELA. Good-bye, and don't bear me rancour.

DON LORENZO. Bear you rancour! I?

DOÑA ANGELA. Then good-bye.

SCENE V

DON LORENZO. [*Seated at table in profound dejection. Fire burns redly, room enveloped in deep shadow. Pause.*] Now I am alone. How the shadows play around me! The fire burns dull and red. So much the better. Darkness gathers. Come to my aid, obscurity! 'Tis now the hour when the conscience spreads its most luminous rays. I would do what is right, but then, I know not what is right. My will is strong enough, but reason is dimmed. Three names dance before my eyes in the black night that enshrouds me. Ángela, Juana, and Inés! Destiny leads me to my Calvary, and I ascend my cross of suffering without complaint. But you, my dear ones, you, Inés, why must you precede me, marking with your tears the way that is to tear my feet? I alone—but not you! My God, my God! how low the flame of conscience flickers, and how faint is my will! Despair, alas! holds me in its grip. I desire good, and seek it in Thee, O Lord. Come to my aid, answer to my call. Shadows that encircle me, space in which I most dolorously wander, time that is mine own eternity of pain, and thou, august silence, that dost hear me in thy consoling mood, call all of you upon your God whom my voice may not reach. Tell him that I would my daughter were spared, and that I implore the chalice of bitterness may pass her by, that I myself may drain it with my lips to the very dregs. Let all fall upon me, and let her live in all her loveliness and goodness and purity. —Not on her, my God, not on her! [*Drops his head on table in bitter weeping.*]

SCENE VI

Don Lorenzo and Juana, who stands in door R.

DON LORENZO. A flickering shadow has passed before my eyes. Has it all been a dream? No, Juana is yonder, and the proof, the proof. [*Opens desk and takes out paper.*] Here is the proof. Unhappily it is no dream. It is terrible and implacable reality. I have read it a hundred times, and can never weary of reading it: 'I have loved you like a son, although you are no child of ours.' 'Although you are no child of ours!'

JUANA. [*Aside, watching him.*] He is reading—reading that letter written by one he believed to be his mother. I it is who am his mother—not another. [*Advances slowly.*] How sad he looks! and there are tears in his eyes. In his eyes, do I say? Perhaps it is my own eyes, looking at him, that are wet. His eyes or mine! What matter? There are tears somewhere. [*Comes nearer.*] He is crying. Why? Because I am his mother? But what of that, if nobody else knows my secret? I am so near death! Yes, death! I shall soon die. Cold and eternal night has already penetrated to the depths of my being. It is all dark within. [*Staggers and leans against the table. Don Lorenzo turns to her.*]

DON LORENZO. Juana!

JUANA. Still that name.

DON LORENZO. Mother!

JUANA. It offends you that I am such—I see it.

DON LORENZO. Do you think so ill of me?

JUANA. Well, if it does not offend you, you are ashamed of me as your mother?

DON LORENZO. I ashamed of you! To-morrow the world will know that I am your son.

JUANA. To-morrow! What do you mean? [*With terror.*] My hearing is dull, and I cannot rightly have understood what you said.

DON LORENZO. I made a mistake. Not to-morrow. You must leave Spain first, and then, when you are in some safe place, since man's justice can often be very cruel, I will proclaim the truth aloud. I will give up a name that is not mine, as well as an appropriated fortune. That is what I have decided to do.

JUANA. Christ above!

DON LORENZO. And then along with Ángela and my poor child I will join you.

JUANA. You, poor and dishonoured, with only a stained and contemptible name! And why? Wherefore? What compels you? Speak, my son. My wits forsake me. What forces you to it?

DON LORENZO. Conscience, mother, and your misdoing.

JUANA. You intend to tell the truth?

DON LORENZO. [*Angrily.*] Why did you ever tell it to me? If I had known nothing about it I should not now be obliged to break my daughter's heart.

JUANA. Why? And you can ask me that? You don't understand? Oh, ungrateful son! [*Hides her face in her hands and sobs bitterly.*]

DON LORENZO. Mother!

JUANA. Because I was dying, because I am dying—and I wanted you to know all that I had sacrificed for your sake before I went. And because I wished to hear you call me mother at least once. For that, and for no other reason. Because the heart within me rose to my throat and nearly choked me, till at last I could no longer command myself, and had to call you son.

DON LORENZO. I understand, mother, and do not blame you.

JUANA. But you will not do as you have just threatened? Say you will not. It would be infamous to your family and most cruel to me.

DON LORENZO. Cruel, yes, but not infamous. With this cruelty shall I wipe out all infamy.

JUANA. Lorenzo!

DON LORENZO. Forgive me.

JUANA. [*Tragically.*] You accuse me of having committed an infamy?

DON LORENZO. I have not said it.

JUANA. [*In stifled voice.*] But it was for your sake—for your sake, my son. [*Don Lorenzo remains silent and gloomy, not looking toward his mother.*] My God, I did it for his sake, and this is how he repays me! Lorenzo!

DON LORENZO. Wrong may not prevail. The work of iniquity must fall into ruins beneath its own weight. My sacrifice will serve to wipe out your sin.

JUANA. Lorenzo! [*Don Lorenzo draws her to the light and places the letter in her hand, obliging her to read it.*]

DON LORENZO. What does it say there?

JUANA. [*Sits down and reads with difficulty.*] 'Forgive me, and may God inspire you.'

DON LORENZO. Well, mother, I have forgiven her, and prayed to Heaven for inspiration. Your entreaties are vain.

SCENE VII

Juana, Don Lorenzo, Doña Angela enters door R.

DOÑA ANGELA. [*Standing in doorway.*] Lorenzo, Inés wants you.

DON LORENZO. My daughter! I am coming. Excuse me, mother. I will return instantly.

JUANA. [*Detains him and speaks softly.*] Now I know that you despise me; now I know that you hate me.

DON LORENZO. Mother!

JUANA. [*Grasps his arm.*] But not for my sake, for hers —for the sake of that dear child.

DON LORENZO. [*Despairingly.*] Not even for her sake.

JUANA. [*Falls into the arm-chair and covers her face with her hands. Exeunt Don Lorenzo and Doña Ángela.*]

SCENE VIII

JUANA. [*Holding the paper in her hand.*] Not even for her sake! [*Sobs.*] Sacrifice yourself, Juana, for your son. Renounce his caresses, tear your breast with your nails on seeing him kiss another woman and call her mother; drink deeply of the tears of bitterness, and gather them in your heart until it overflows or bursts. Bear the brand of shame upon your brow, wear yourself out in poverty and sorrow in a garret for twenty years, with no other happiness or consolation than seeing him pass in his carriage from the distance. Oh, heavens, I am dying! [*Pause. She gets better.*] Still,—still worse,—poor Juana! suffer all I have mentioned, and in exchange procure him wealth, reputation, celebrity—and at the last moment of your life come to him and only ask a kiss, only ask him to say once: 'How good you have been to me! How fondly you have loved me!' What will he say? Nothing of this. He will glance at you in austere sadness, and tell you that you have committed an infamy, and that he must wipe out your crime,—that your work is—a work of iniquity. A work of iniquity! Oh, Lorenzo, my son! Why are you so cruel? Why do you cast from you in contempt all that I gave you at the price of my own happiness? See what tears you cost me! [*Changes her voice and crosses R. with a desperate gesture.*] And my sacrifice has been in vain. I have forfeited my own happiness and lost his too. Mad woman, egoist! Why did I tell him the truth? [*Pause.*] But it must not be, it must not be. No, the work of iniquity will not fall into ruins yet a while. Poor visionary! I will deny everything. [*In a dead voice.*] You will be happy and rich and powerful whether you like it or no. He put the sole proof into my hand. [*Takes up the paper.*] Very well, then. Between his mother and his daughter he will be saved. Strange coincidence! She, calling for him, obliges him to go away, and I stay behind. Ah, let us exhaust what little strength remains. So, a little nearer still, through the darkness—just so dark a night was it when my mistress came to my bedside and murmuring asked: 'Would you have your child rich and happy?' And first I doubted, and then I consented—and now—and now I still say 'yes.' [*Reaches table. Pause.*] Is Lorenzo coming back? [*Listens.*] Yes, I think he is coming. He will ask me for the letter as he did before. Here, to the fire with it. [*Tries to walk, but cannot.*] I hear his voice. Strength fails me. I have no time. He will come. No, I will not give it up. Once more it is in my hands. Ah, now I know, now I know. I will slip a clean sheet into the envelope so that he may notice nothing. [*Does this.*] Lorenzo calls it a work of iniquity. My poor boy, he is in some things as innocent as a child. Thus—thus, I leave it where it was—and this other goes to the flames. [*Throws paper into the fire and stoops to watch it burn.*] Now it is in flames. See how luminously they quiver upon my mistress's portrait. [*Looks at portrait upon the wall.*] And now, see, it is in ashes—that which was the only proof. The only one? No: another still remains—it is I—and soon that also will be ashes. [*Pause.*] Now I will go to my room. [*Moves.*] My God, how weak I have grown! [*Moves again with an effort.*] But I have saved him. Felicity, fortune are his—I cannot see,—I cannot see. The light is dim. Is it the light or my eyes that are dim? [*Approaches table, takes up candle and walks again.*] Light, light! where is my room? Shadows! All is darkness. Alas, alas, I cannot, I cannot. [*Lets candle fall. Room is only lit by the red reflection of the fire. She falls between fireplace and table.*]

SCENE IX

Juana, Duchess, Don Lorenzo, Doña Ángela, and Inés. The latter enters R. Don Lorenzo tries to get away from his daughter, who stands at door in white; behind her, half hidden by curtains, the Duchess and Doña Ángela.

DON LORENZO. [*Coming down the stage.*] No more, no more. It is the last test,—the last, yes. But, oh, how my will fainted.

DOÑA ÁNGELA. [*To Inés.*] Follow him. Do not leave him alone. He will give in.

INÉS. Why do you fly from me, father? [*Advances a little, behind her the duchess and Doña Ángela. This scene must be strongly marked and fantastic. Don Lorenzo, in the middle of the stage, evinces in his attitude, manner, and expression that he is undergoing a desperate inward struggle. Inés, delicate-looking and charming, approaches him slowly, and Doña Ángela and duchess, in black, follow, encouraging her. Juana dying; the study is quite dark save for the glimmer of the firelight which shows out Inés sharply.*]

DON LORENZO. Here lies my real temptation. Oh, how lovely she is! What an aureola of divine beauty encircles her head—the sole ray of light in this heavy darkness.

DOÑA ÁNGELA. [*Aside to Inés.*] Do you see? He cannot resist you. Implore him, implore him, my child.

INÉS. [*Advancing.*] Kiss me, father.

DON LORENZO. [*Retreating.*] Alas for me if those dear arms should clasp themselves like a halter round my neck!

JUANA. [*Aside.*] A halter round the neck! He is right.

INÉS. For the love of God, father, for the love of me, for all the tears shed by those eyes you used to kiss so fondly when I was a child. [*Lifts her hands to her eyes, and then offers them to Don Lorenzo to kiss.*] See how the drops still flow from my eyelids. My fingers are wet with them. Kiss them, and let your lips taste of their bitterness.

DON LORENZO. Yes—I will kiss them—I will kiss them —but, alas! if one of mine should fall upon them.

JUANA. [*Aside.*] Fall, fall, so he said. I also am falling into the bottomless abyss. But first, first I must embrace my son.

INÉS. Father [*Don Lorenzo retreats. Doña Ángela, Inés and the duchess follow him.*]

DOÑA ÁNGELA. Lorenzo!

JUANA. 'Twas Lorenzo they called. There—there—I see something.

DON LORENZO. No, no—a thousand times, no. Would you degrade me?

INÉS. And you, father—who would believe it?—would kill me. If not, why do you seek to place an obstacle between me and the love of my life?

DON LORENZO. No, my Inés, no—the duchess—it is the duchess.

INÉS. It is not true. The duchess consents.

DON LORENZO. At the cost of my honour.

DUCHESS. Not so, Inés. In exchange for silence.

INÉS. Don't you hear her, father?

DON LORENZO. [*Moving away and repulsing her.*] I only hear voices begging my conscience of me. I only see shadows pursuing me through the shadows—phantasms of space, engendered by temptation. Leave me, leave me—in God's name. If you are strong enough to wring my heart, at least you are not strong enough to bend my will.

JUANA. His voice! Lorenzo, Lorenzo! [*Comes over to embrace him.*]

DON LORENZO. Mother! [*Embraces her.*]

INÉS. [*Taking refuge behind Doña Ángela.*] Whose voice is that? Who is that woman? What shade is that which has come out of the darkness and encircles my father with its arms? I'm afraid.

DON LORENZO. Juana! my mother!

INÉS. His mother! Why does he call her mother?

DON LORENZO. Because she's my mother, and because I should call her so.

JUANA. I? his mother? Good gracious, what an idea! How I wish it were so!

DUCHESS. Do you hear—do you hear what she says?

DOÑA ÁNGELA. She denies it.

DON LORENZO. [*Violently.*] You are my mother.

JUANA. Ah, my poor Lorenzo. [*Laughs with an effort, embraces him, and whispers.*] Child of my heart!

DON LORENZO. On your life, repeat aloud what you have just whispered to me.

JUANA. I whispered! Well, what did I say? To be his mother! Could I wish for a greater blessing?

DON LORENZO. [*Furiously.*] Ah, you deny it.

DOÑA ÁNGELA. Lorenzo!

DON LORENZO. [*With increasing fury.*] Do you deny that you are my mother?

JUANA. Why not?

DON LORENZO. [*Despairingly.*] You denied me at the hour of my birth, and again you deny me at the hour of your death.

JUANA. [*Clasping him closely, so that in the darkness it is not possible to discern if they are embracing, or if Don Lorenzo has caught her in his rage.*] Child of my love! [*Whispers in a dying voice.*]

DON LORENZO. [*Deliriously.*] That's so, that's so.

JUANA. I am dying.

DON LORENZO. No, mother.

DUCHESS. Heavens! Is the man going to kill her? Help! [*Runs to door R.*]

DOÑA ÁNGELA. Edward—doctor!

DON LORENZO. Mother, mother!

JUANA. No,—God help me!—no, not that.

SCENE X

Don Lorenzo, Juana, Inés, Doña Ángela, Duchess, Dr. Tomás, and Edward. Latter two enter R. with lights, all help to separate Juana and Don Lorenzo.

DR. TOMÁS. Come, come.

DON LORENZO. My mother — forgive me, forgive me. You don't wish me to call you mother—my mother.

JUANA. Farewell.

DON LORENZO. Juana! [*Juana makes a terrible effort, and rises as if wounded in the heart by the name of Juana; falls back.*]

DR. TOMÁS. Dead!

DON LORENZO. No, it cannot be. [*Embraces her.*] I killed her by calling her mother,—and the last cry she heard from my lips was Juana. Ah, my God, my God! Why hast thou punished her so hardly, and why hast thou forsaken me?

ACT III

SCENE—*Same as previous Acts*

SCENE I

Dr. Tomás. Afterwards servant.

DR. TOMÁS. Everything is quiet. The girl's sobbing can no longer be heard, and Don Lorenzo's fury is calmed. 'Tis but the gentle precursor of a fresh tempest. [*Pause.*] There are moments when I doubt and vacillate. He,—he,—my good friend, poor Lorenzo—the very idea gives me no rest. Well, well, we shall soon know the truth now,—meanwhile, courage. I have sacred obligations to fulfil towards this afflicted family. Nobody could more earnestly desire to help them than I.

SERVANT. A gentleman, accompanied by two—really sir, I don't know what to call them—but their dress,—well, the gentleman has given me his card for you, and they are all waiting outside.

DR. TOMÁS. [*Looking at card.*] Ah, Doctor Bermúdez. Show him in.

SERVANT. And the other two?

DR. TOMÁS. Let them wait. [*Exit servant.*] As the hour approaches my doubts and my anxiety increase. Poor Doña Ángela! what a blow for her! And in what a state of nervous agitation is her unhappy daughter! How lucid her glance, and how quick her intelligence!

Nobody has explained the matter to her, and yet I believe she knows everything. She guesses what she does not precisely know, and suspects what she does not guess. Oh, no; the situation cannot be prolonged. However sad reality may be, we have to face it.

SCENE II

Dr. Tomás, Dr. Bermúdez. Afterwards two keepers, attired like gentlemen, but evincing that they are not such. Dr. Tomás advances with outstretched hand.

DR. TOMÁS. Doctor.

BERMÚDEZ. Dr. Tomás.

DR. TOMÁS. Punctual as ever.

BERMÚDEZ. No, I am a little early. I want to hide these fellows somewhere.

DR. TOMÁS. Yes, yes, I understand.

BERMÚDEZ. I have made them dress so as to avert suspicion in Don Lorenzo. This is a case for such general precautions.

DR. TOMÁS. Quite so, quite so. We must proceed with great caution. It was an access of fury, a veritable access of fury, as I told you. He has only had one, the other night. Perhaps I am mistaken.

BERMÚDEZ. I sincerely hope so—and you, too, I am sure.

DR. TOMÁS. Ah, my friend, I scarce know what I am doing. But we trust in your science, your experience, and profound penetration to relieve us of our present doubt.

BERMÚDEZ. You flatter me. You also are a doctor——

DR. TOMÁS. Don't count on me, Bermúdez. I am good

for nothing. I declare myself incompetent. It is a question of my best friend, of a brother almost. Besides, he has always struck me—you know my school. There is not a divisional line between reason and madness.

BERMÚDEZ. Quite true. All men of learning are more or less insane.

DR. TOMÁS. Precisely. Excitement of the brain beyond certain limits——

BERMÚDEZ. That's it. What we have to do is to see what can be done with Don Lorenzo. Now these two fellows——

DR. TOMÁS. Oh, it will be easy enough to invent a tale. We'll call them witnesses—say they've come with the notary—anything, in fact. Poor Lorenzo is not in a condition to take note of details.

BERMÚDEZ. Where will they wait?

DR. TOMÁS. [*Pointing to door R.*] Inside that door.

BERMÚDEZ. [*Going up the stage.*] Here, Braulio!
[*Enter two keepers, rather heavy and rough in appearance.*]

DR. TOMÁS. Go into that closet. You will be called if necessary,—meanwhile, remain quiet. [*Keepers salute and enter closet R.*] Since Juana's death Don Lorenzo has not used this room. [*To Bermúdez.*] With the door shut—— [*Shuts it.*]

BERMÚDEZ. [*Looking at his watch.*] I will be with you in a moment. I'll be back again before the notary arrives. I'm only off somewhere in the neighbourhood.

DR. TOMÁS. A visit?

BERMÚDEZ. Yes; a very strange case of insanity. [*Enter Doña Ángela C., who stands looking at Bermúdez.*] She's——? [*To Dr. Tomás, glancing at Doña Ángela.*]

DR. TOMÁS. Yes—his wife. Don't say anything to her.

BERMÚDEZ. [*Aside to Dr. Tomás.*] I'll be back shortly. Your servant, madam. [*Salutes Doña Ángela, and exit C.*]

SCENE III

Doña Ángela and Dr. Tomás. Doña Ángela follows Bermúdez with her eyes, then glances towards the closet where keepers are concealed.

DOÑA ÁNGELA. Who was that going away? And who were the two men that accompanied him.

DR. TOMÁS. Don't be alarmed, dear madam. It will be all right. These are only ordinary precautions, for, who knows? Don Lorenzo might have another access of fury like that of the night before last, and for your sakes— for his own——

DOÑA ÁNGELA. Oh, doctor, don't hint such a thing.

DR. TOMÁS. Don't you remember with what frenzy he grasped poor Juana's dying body? Now that nobody is listening, in all confidence let me say that I firmly believe he was the determining cause——

DOÑA ÁNGELA. Tomás, Tomás!

Dr. TOMÁS. Well, at any rate he hastened her death. You heard how bitterly he accused himself in his delirium. Don't let us forge illusions. It was a real access of——

DOÑA ÁNGELA. [*Sobbing.*] Lorenzo, my husband!

DR. TOMÁS. The crisis may return, for to-day——

DOÑA ÁNGELA. Yes, I know what his intention is. Ah, doctor, how unfortunate we are! How unfortunate my poor Lorenzo is!

DR. TOMÁS. What is he doing now?

Doña Ángela. He is quite calm. He writes, and walks about. He wants to be continually with Inés and me, because solitude terrifies him. A moment ago he stared at me mournfully, but with such tenderness, and kissed me, murmuring, 'poor Ángela.'

Dr. Tomás. You must not contradict him.

Doña Ángela. No, doctor. We agree with him in everything.

Dr. Tomás. And he still persists in the same idea?

Doña Ángela. Yes. From time to time he asks what o'clock it is, gets impatient with the notary's delay, and then mutters in an undertone: 'Though all the world should oppose me, I must do it.'

Dr. Tomás. What a fellow! What character!

Doña Ángela. Oh, doctor, for the love of God, don't deceive me. Tell me, do you really believe Lorenzo to be —to be,—no, I can't—I can't bring myself to pronounce the horrible word.

Dr. Tomás. I don't yet know what to believe. We shall soon see, my dear friend, we shall see. It was precisely to be relieved once and for all of intolerable anxiety that I asked Dr. Bermúdez to call. He is the first authority upon all such cases.

Doña Ángela. But it is impossible, it is surely impossible.

Dr. Tomás. It would rejoice me to learn so, and we need not lose hope. But impossible, madam! Ah, human reason is so slight a thing.

Doña Ángela. Oh, my dear husband! No, I cannot bear—it cannot be.

Dr. Tomás. Come, come, Doña Ángela. Have sense and courage, if only for your daughter's sake, for poor Inés.

And who knows yet? We have to see if Don Lorenzo has any explanation to offer—any proof——

DOÑA ÁNGELA. What proof can he have? Even the dying Juana cried out to him, 'No, no, you are not my son,' while he, frenzied and delirious, grasped her in his arms and strove to force an impossible confession from the half dead body, calling her 'mother' in the strident voice of dementia. No, you can't console me, friend. It is useless. I foresee that our misfortune is inevitable.

DR. TOMÁS. I almost fear so.

DOÑA ÁNGELA. And then his way of receiving the duchess, he who is always the pink of courtesy, a finished gentleman——

DR. TOMÁS. You are right. On that occasion I understood how it was with him. But who can be resigned when fate strikes so suddenly?

DOÑA ÁNGELA. Adoring a child as he adores Inés, is there anybody who could act as he proposes to act to-day?

DR. TOMÁS. Nobody, madam, nobody in his right mind.

DOÑA ÁNGELA. Have you told Dr. Bermúdez?

DR. TOMÁS. Not everything. That would be dangerous. But quite enough to enable him to pronounce an opinion.

DOÑA ÁNGELA. And what is it?

DR. TOMÁS. Am I to speak fully?

DOÑA ÁNGELA. Yes, yes, doctor. Conceal nothing. I know there is no remedy.

DR. TOMÁS. With skilful treatment, separated from everybody, especially from those whose presence could only serve to exasperate his nervous sensibility by very reason of his affection for them——

Doña Ángela. Tomás!

Dr. Tomás. In some good asylum here in Spain or abroad——

Doña Ángela. What! What is it you say? Separate him from us! Take him away! He—he—never. I am his wife. I will never consent to it.

Dr. Tomás. The sight of Inés will aggravate his delirium.

Doña Ángela. Her absence would be his death.

Dr. Tomás. He smothered that poor woman to death.

Doña Ángela. There you are wrong, Tomás. With her father Inés runs no risk. She is his daughter.

Dr. Tomás. He believed Juana to be his mother.

Doña Ángela. It must not be, Tomás, it must not be. Why can't you find a way of relieving my anguish instead of torturing me so?

Dr. Tomás. Doña Ángela!

Doña Ángela. It is true, my friend, 'twould indeed be no easy matter to find consolation for such a sorrow as mine.

Dr. Tomás. There is no human sorrow inconsolable, however great it may be.

Doña Ángela. Oh, but mine is.

Dr. Tomás. Yours still less than many others. Come, let us discuss it dispassionately.

Doña Ángela. How can I, with fever running fire in my veins?

Dr. Tomás. Hear me out. If what Don Lorenzo asserts be true, if there were irrefragable proofs——

Doña Ángela. Then my poor husband would not be out

of his mind. We it would be who are blind and foolish. Oh, what a blessing that would be!

DR. TOMÁS. Not so great, for in that case you would have to face poverty, dishonour—death even.

DOÑA ÁNGELA. Hush, Tomás.

DR. TOMÁS. I say death advisedly, for Inés would most certainly die of it. On the other hand, if Lorenzo's calamity be proved——

DOÑA ÁNGELA. Don't continue. I can't bear to think of it.

DR. TOMÁS. But think of Inés, and in thinking of her you will see that, terrible as the wound is—we must acknowledge the fact, sad as it is—it is by no means a mortal wound. For youth, what alone is mortal is to destroy the future—not simply precipitate the past into nothingness.

DOÑA ÁNGELA. For mercy's sake, Tomás!

DR. TOMÁS. The happiness of Inés' lifetime depends upon her father's calamity—don't forget it.

DOÑA ÁNGELA. Let God's will be done, but do not seek to awaken ideas rather fitted to frighten than to comfort me.

SCENE IV

Ángela, Dr. Tomás, Don Lorenzo R.

DON LORENZO. [*Aside.*] But where have I left the key? Oh, my head! and the notary will be here presently. I left the letter in the desk. I remember quite well. Two days ago, when my mother——

DR. TOMÁS. [*Without seeing Don Lorenzo.*] Poor Doña Ángela! The proof [ordeal] will be a terrible one.

DON LORENZO. What? What are they saying? The

proof! yes; they are speaking of the proof. [*Looks eagerly about the table for key of desk.*]

DOÑA ÁNGELA. Yes, it will be a terrible one—very terrible to walk between two precipices. Lorenzo on the one side, Inés on the other. You are right indeed.

DON LORENZO. [*Aloud, angrily.*] I have lost it.

DR TOMÁS. [*Aside, turning round.*] I should think you have, unfortunate man.

DOÑA ÁNGELA. Lorenzo!

DON LORENZO. Ah, they're there. [*Recognises them with a suspicious glance.*]

DOÑA ÁNGELA. [*Gently.*] What are you looking for? We will help you.

DON LORENZO. You! no. Wherefore? It is my work.

DOÑA ÁNGELA. But at least tell us what you have lost.

DON LORENZO. Everything—even the love of mine own. Say if there can be more for me to lose.

DOÑA ÁNGELA. No, Lorenzo, do not believe it.

DON LORENZO. At last! The key. Heaven be praised! [*Aside, distrustfully.*] It was there—it was in the lock. [*Opens desk and takes out the paper Juana placed there.*] Ah, here it is. I breathe again freely. [*Reads.*] 'For Lorenzo.' This is the paper.

DOÑA ÁNGELA. [*Approaching.*] Have you found what you were looking for?

DON LORENZO. Yes. [*Dr. Tomás also approaches.*]

DOÑA ANGELA. What paper is it?
[*Don Lorenzo makes a movement to take paper out of envelope, but seeing Dr. Tomás and Doña Angela come nearer, he puts it back in desk, locks it, and pockets the key.*]

Don Lorenzo. A very important one. [*Looks from one to the other angrily and suspiciously.*] But why do you want to know?

Doña Ángela. Don't be offended, Lorenzo. Forgive me if I have committed an indiscretion.

Don Lorenzo. I forgive! It is I who want your forgiveness. Through me, through my fault, are you about to be plunged into misery.

Doña Ángela. Do not say so. We could never be miserable, you being happy.

Don Lorenzo. And I, could I be happy, fortune having deserted you and my beloved child?

Doña Ángela. She, too, will be happy.

Don Lorenzo. Impossible, for you know what I am thinking of.

Doña Ángela. You have told me. Don't you remember?

Don Lorenzo. [*To Dr. Tomás.*] And you?

Dr Tomás. I also know.

Don Lorenzo. You approve?

Doña Ángela. [*Sweetly.*] Whatever you do will be well done.

Don Lorenzo. [*To Dr. Tomás*] What have you to say?

Dr. Tomás. The same.

Don Lorenzo. [*Thoughtfully.*] 'The same.' What conformity of opinion! Do you know that I have sent for a notary?

Doña Ángela. We know it.

Don Lorenzo. [*Looking at both.*] You know it. And do you likewise know that I am about to have a legal act drawn up containing my formal declaration and renunciation?

DOÑA ÁNGELA. Yes, Lorenzo.

DON LORENZO. So that the judge may then ordain as the law directs? Is it not so?

DR. TOMÁS. It is natural.

DON LORENZO. [*To Doña Ángela.*] What do you say to it?

DOÑA ÁNGELA. [*In weeping voice.*] If this wealth we now enjoy is not legally yours—you do well.

DR. TOMÁS. If the name you bear is not yours, you must certainly give it up.

DOÑA ÁNGELA. In any case your will is law.

DON LORENZO. Yes, but a tyrannical law, an impious law —eh?

DOÑA ÁNGELA. Still, a law that I respect above all others.

DON LORENZO. [*Nervous, unquiet, almost irritable.*] And you don't resist it? You don't struggle against it?

DR. TOMÁS. Your conduct is that of a man of honour. Strictly speaking, there is nothing else for you to do.

DON LORENZO. What unheard-of submission! What extraordinary docility! What a sudden change! You are deceiving me. I tell you, you are lying to me. [*Violently.*]

DOÑA ÁNGELA. For pity's sake, Lorenzo.

DR. TOMÁS. [*Aside.*] Ah, there is no hope. Like a black wave dementia has spread over his mind.

DON LORENZO. [*More calmly.*] Well, well, better so. [*Pause. Approaches Doña Ángela affectionately.*] Where is Inés?

DOÑA ANGELA. My poor child!

DON LORENZO. You don't defend her against me? [*Then gently.*] Nevertheless, it is your duty.

DOÑA ÁNGELA. Alas, Lorenzo, what strength has your wretched wife to use against you? Your will grows iron in strife and calamity; mine bends to the very dust.

DON LORENZO. You are right. My will is irresistible when duty orders me. [*To Dr. Tomás.*] What do you think of all this?

DR. TOMÁS. That it should be so.

DON LORENZO. So it is. [*Pause.*] Poor Ángela! And do you know what we are going to do once the act is signed and the proof given up?

DR. TOMÁS. You have a proof?

DON LORENZO. You didn't know. [*Aside, wondering.*] (And they were talking about it when I entered!) Yes, I have it, irrefutable, past doubt, clear as daylight, although it is black as night and treason.

DOÑA ÁNGELA. Keep calm, Lorenzo.

DR. TOMÁS. Then what is it?

DON LORENZO. A letter of my mother's—of the woman who called herself my mother.

DOÑA ÁNGELA. [*Aside.*] Good Heavens! Can it be true?

DON LORENZO. Her signature, her handwriting—it is here —in my power.

DR. TOMÁS. [*Aside.*] Ah, if it were so.

DON LORENZO. Then when the proof is delivered up, you, my poor Inés, and I will at once leave this house—this house which already has ceased to be ours, and which this very day the law will take into possession until it is handed over to the heirs of Avendaña. [*With increasing animation.*] And in a little while we shall wander forth without resources, without a name, bearing a dying child in our arms—for have you not assured us that Inés will die? [*to Dr. Tomás*]—fronting a despairing solitude——no, 'twas not well said—I blasphemed. We will bear away with us an unstained honour and a tranquil conscience, and our heads will be held high, while God is with us. What matter if the world forsake us, thus accompanied?

DOÑA ÁNGELA. [*Embracing him.*] Before, I said with my lips only: 'Your will is law, Lorenzo.' Now I say it with my heart.

DR. TOMÁS. [*Aside.*] If the proof exists, this man is a saint. But, alas! if it does not exist, the unfortunate fellow is nothing but a lunatic. [*Enter servant.*]

SERVANT. The Duchess of Almonte, and his Grace the Duke.

DOÑA ÁNGELA. Show them in. [*To Dr. Tomás.*] Have you informed them?

DR. TOMÁS. [*To Doña Ángela.*] I told them last night. The duchess promised to come. You see, she has kept her word.

DON LORENZO. I cannot see them. I must be alone, unless you are with me—only you. Good-bye, Ángela.

DOÑA ÁNGELA. Good-bye, Lorenzo.

DON LORENZO. [*Looking at his watch.*] How slowly time passes! [*Goes to door R. Dr. Tomás follows him.*] Have you given notice to the witnesses? [*At door.*]

DR. TOMÁS. I have two inside waiting, and another will be here presently.

DON LORENZO. Who are they?

DR. TOMÁS. You don't know them. They are friends of mine.

Don Lorenzo. And why not mine too?

Dr. Tomás. I always considered my friends as yours.

Don Lorenzo. [*Looks at him for a moment.*] So they are. [*Aside.*] Ah, this complaisance! I would have preferred to see them resist—struggle against me!

SCENE V

Doña Angela, the Duchess, Edward, and Dr. Tomás.

Doña Ángela. Duchess!

Duchess. Madam! [*Salutes affectionately.*]

Doña Ángela. You are always so good to us.

Duchess. It is my duty to offer the consolations of sincere friendship in your cruel trouble. God has willed that the same misfortune should strike us all though in different ways. [*Lowers her voice and points to Edward on uttering the last word.*]

Doña Ángela. But what then do you call the misfortune that has struck me? I know not.

Edward. Well, madam, the moment for naming it has arrived. It is called poverty, and shame, and the death of Inés, or——

Doña Ángela *and* Duchess, [*At same time.*] Edward!

Edward. Forgive me, mother. We should each and all speak out the truth to-day. You have already said: 'I will compromise with Don Lorenzo's calamity for the sake of the love I bear you and that which you bear me; but I will never compromise with his public dishonour,—never, not even for the price of your life.' My life, mother, was it not so 'twas said?

Duchess. [*With energy, but sadly.*] Yes.

EDWARD. [*Going toward Doña Angela.*] Then, madam, let us probe the misfortune that has struck you. Whether is it called dishonour or madness? This is the problem we have to solve. Should Don Lorenzo be correct, should he be in his sound senses, should there be proof forthcoming of his assertion, it is for us to respect his cruel virtue. But if, as I (by a thousand signs that almost constitute evidence) believe, an eternal cloud has dimmed his intellect, and the light of his reason is for ever quenched,—then defend yourself, Doña Ángela. It is your most sacred duty. Defend the name you bear, your social position, even Don Lorenzo's honour, against his own raving; defend,—why should I keep it back? —Inés' life and her life's felicity. Do not, madam, leave such almighty interests and so dear an object at the mercy of a madman.

DUCHESS. Edward!

EDWARD. The word is a harsh one, but the time has come to pronounce it. Once for all, let us learn the fact whether this battle for reputation and existence into which Don Lorenzo has cast us is what it seems or what I fear:—whether, finally, the heroic sacrifice of this implacable scholar is insanity or sanctity.

DUCHESS. Enough, Edward. [*Doña Ángela sits down on sofa, weeping bitterly. Duchess goes over to her.*]

DR. TOMÁS. [*To Edward.*] The happiness of this family affects me as closely as my own. What you propose to do has already been considered, and both the law and science will be called in to decide.

DUCHESS. I hope to Heaven the darkness will be illuminated for you. [*To Doña Ángela.*] Come, come, madam: courage, resignation! Where is Inés?

DOÑA ÁNGELA. Do you wish to see her?

DUCHESS. Yes.

DOÑA ÁNGELA. Come, then. [*To Dr. Tomás.*] And you too. I would like you to see her. For the past three days fever alone has lent her strength. My daughter, my dear child is very ill.

DR. TOMÁS. Poor girl!
[*Exeunt Doña Ángela, Duchess, and Dr. Tomás.*]

SCENE VI

EDWARD. They persist in doubting. What blindness! They can't understand that the unfortunate gentleman, from force of seeking, not the righting of wrongs, like the Errant Knight, but the reason of all the varied rights invented by the accumulated wisdom of centuries, has ended by losing the only one that Providence saw fit to bestow upon him—namely, natural reason. Oh, but this must not be. I cannot allow them to sacrifice my dear one's life to the extravagances of a poor madman.

SCENE VII

Edward, Inés, comes out by closet R., where the keepers are concealed, agitated, and as if fleeing.

INÉS. What are those men? Who are they?

EDWARD. [*Rushing towards her.*] Inés, my beloved! How pale you are! Your divine glance is hemmed round by deep purple shadow.

INÉS. But answer me. Who are they? What are they waiting for? Send them away. [*Approaches the door cautiously and peeps in; Edward endeavours to lead her down the stage.*] There is something sinister about them. My father—where is my father? I was looking for him between the drawing-room and yonder closet, and I saw them—I can't bear the sight of them, and yet I cannot take my eyes from off them.

EDWARD. But what is the matter with you, dearest? Why do your eyes seem to shun me? Is it from me that you are running away? Inés, have you wearied of my love?

INÉS. [*Coming down the stage.*] Wearied of your love? You must know that it is my life. But oh, Edward, to what a frightful ordeal fate has subjected us! You do not understand it. For me supreme bliss lies in your love, and the hope I place in your love is a still greater bliss—a far, far greater. The one is our present, the other contains all our future. And yet, Edward, dearest, that same hope has now become a crime for your Inés, yes, a crime. Can a cruelty more exquisite be conceived? That which destiny denies no other living being it denies me. Yesterday I was but a child. My thoughts floated upon laughter in a sphere of white transparency, like a vapoury mist in moonlight. To-day they are as heavy as lead, as burning as lava. Could you but hear their horrible whispers in the silence of night. And these thoughts are not mine. It is not my will that gives them birth. They come I know not whence. I cast them from me, and still they return. They vex me with chiding complaints: 'your poor father,' one moment, and then assail me with tempting voices, murmuring: 'Inés, Inés, who knows?—you may yet be happy—love may yet smile upon you—hope, hope, poor little thing.' Can you think of anything more horrible—surely it must be my bad angel—than to hear within oneself the voice of Satan whispering of hope to one bidden to say farewell to it?

EDWARD. You are not yourself, my dear Inés.

INÉS. [*Approaching Edward.*] I am filled with remorse.

EDWARD. For what?

INÉS. I don't know. I have done nothing wrong. My father! My poor father!

EDWARD. You angel of my life, my heart's desire, be calm, be calm. I beg of you to spare yourself.

INÉS. Whisper, Edward. I could almost wish I were dead.

SCENE VIII

Don Lorenzo, Inés, and Edward. Don Lorenzo enters C., and stands listening to Inés.

DON LORENZO. [*Aside.*] Dead, she said?

EDWARD. You dead! No, Inés, don't say such a thing.

INÉS. Why not? If I do not die of sorrow—should fortune ever again smile upon me, then must I die of remorse.

DON LORENZO. [*Aside.*] Of remorse! She! Should fortune ever again smile upon her! What worse fate floats in the air and hangs threateningly above my head? Remorse!—I have again caught another passing word. I traverse rooms and galleries, and wander from one place to another, pricked by insufferable anguish. I hear talk that I do not understand, and meet glances still further from my comprehension. I see tears here, smiles there, and nobody opposes me,—all either fly from me or watch me. [*Aloud.*] What is this? What is this?

INÉS. [*Rushing to his arms.*] Oh, father!

DON LORENZO. Inés, how white you are? Whence this dolorous constriction of your lips? Why do you essay a smile only to end in sobbing? How lovely she is in her sorrow! And it is all my fault.

INÉS. No, father.

DON LORENZO. I am cruel. Oh, if you do not say it, you think it.

EDWARD. Inés is too sweet-natured to harbour rebellious thoughts. But we who see her suffer cannot help thinking and saying it for her.

DON LORENZO. It is but natural you should do so.

EDWARD. [*Passionately.*] Then if I am right, you are wrong.

DON LORENZO. I am not in the wrong for that. There is something more pallid than the white brow of a lovesick maid; there are tears sadder far than the crystal drops of her beautiful eyes, something still crueller than the curving smiles of her lips, and something yet more tragic than the death of our beloved.

EDWARD. [*With violence and contempt.*] What is this worse pallor, these sadder tears, and still mournfuller tragedies?

DON LORENZO. [*Seizing his arm.*] Madman! The pallor of crime, the tears of remorse, the consciousness of one's own infamy.

EDWARD. And this infamy, this remorse, this crime would lie in furthering your daughter's happiness?

DON LORENZO. [*Despairingly.*] It should not be—but so it is nevertheless. [*Pause.*] And this makes my torment. This is the idea that will drive me mad.

INÉS. No, no, father. You must not say that. Do what you think best without thought of me. What does it matter whether I live or die?

DON LORENZO. Inés!

INÉS. Only, do not be uncertain in it—above all, do not let others see your uncertainty. Let your speech be clear and persuasive, as it is now, and do not let worry blind you. Be calm, father. I implore you by all that is sacred.

Don Lorenzo. What do you mean? I do not understand.

Inés. Do I myself know rightly what I mean? Adieu, adieu. I cannot bear to grieve you.

Edward. [*To Don Lorenzo.*] Alas, if 'twere possible for you to take counsel with your heart, and silence the prompting of thought.

Inés. [*To Edward.*] Do not vex him. Come with me—if you thwart him maybe 'twill force his hate.

Don Lorenzo. Poor child!—she also is struggling—but she will conquer. She is not my daughter for nothing. [*Utters this proudly. Inés and Edward go up the stage; passing the door of the closet, Inés sees the keepers, and makes a movement of horror.*]

Inés. What sinister vision is it that frights my gaze? Those men? Oh, father, do not enter there.

Edward. Come, Inés, come.

Inés. [*To her father.*] No, no. I beseech you, father.

Don Lorenzo. [*Going towards her.*] Inés!

Inés. Those men—there—look! [*Points to closet. Don Lorenzo stands and follows her eyes. At that moment the keepers, hearing her cry, lift the curtain and show themselves.*]

Edward. [*Leading Inés away.*] At last!

SCENE IX

Don Lorenzo, Braulio and Benito. [*Pause.*]

Don Lorenzo. Who can they be? Enter, pray. [*The keepers advance timidly, and speak abruptly.*]

Braulio. Dr. Tomás——

DON LORENZO. [*Aside.*] Ah, I understand.

BENITO. Told us to wait there——

DON LORENZO. Excuse me, I did not know——

BRAULIO. Not at all, sir.

DON LORENZO. [*Aside.*] How odd they look, in sooth. Pray, be seated.

BENITO. Thanks, sir.

BRAULIO. We are well enough standing.

DON LORENZO. I cannot permit it——

BRAULIO. Don't trouble yourself, sir.

BENITO. If the gentleman orders it, it is better to take a seat. [*Both sit down on sofa. Don Lorenzo remains standing.*]

DON LORENZO. [*Aside.*] Their looks seem to bode no good, or is it, perhaps, that my eyes only reflect the flashes that dart across my mind? [*Inspects them again attentively. Aloud.*] It was Miss Avendaña who saw you when she passed, and mentioned it to me.

BRAULIO. Yes, that beautiful young lady.

BENITO. Who looked so sorrowful.

BRAULIO. Like the picture of the Dolorosa. [*The keepers speak shortly, and after these remarks fall into sudden silence, remaining stiff and immovable, looking vaguely before them.*]

DON LORENZO. You frightened her, and she almost ran away at the sight of you. But you must not be astonished. The poor girl is very ill—indeed, she is scarce other than a child yet.

BRAULIO. [*Smiling sillily.*] It always happens to us in every house.

Don Lorenzo. [*Aside, wondering.*] In every house!

Benito. [*Looking for the first time at Don Lorenzo, and again looking steadily in front of him.*] Can she be that poor gentleman's daughter,—eh?

Don Lorenzo. What poor gentleman?

Benito. [*Without looking at him.*] The gentleman who is—— [*Touches his forehead, still not looking at Don Lorenzo, who, unobserved by the keepers, makes a gesture of surprise.*]

Don Lorenzo. [*Aside.*] Ah—no—what an idea! [*Aloud, with an effort of self-control.*] Just so. She is the daughter of—— [*Observes them with increasing anxiety.*]

Benito. Well, she is very beautiful, though so sad.

Braulio. 'Tis reason enough she has to be sad.

Don Lorenzo. You know——?

Braulio. Everything. [*Looks a moment at Don Lorenzo and then away.*]

Don Lorenzo. Dr. Tomás told you?

Benito. Not to us.

Braulio. He told the doctor.

Benito. Why should he talk to us? We, in doing our duty——

Don Lorenzo. [*Aside.*] All my body is bathed in a cold sweat, like the sweat of death. I am raving—This can't possibly be true. [*Repeats mechanically.*] In doing your duty——

Braulio. We are here on the look-out in case he should become obstreperous.

Don Lorenzo. In case he should become obstreperous?—who?

BRAULIO. Why, the gentleman.

DON LORENZO. [*Falls back staring at him in terror; passes his hand over his forehead as if to brush away an idea; retreats still further, staggers, and leans against the table. Then speaks low and abruptly in a dead voice.*] So you know everything.

BRAULIO. Nearly everything.

BENITO. As we have been waiting here for some time, we have heard the servants talk.

DON LORENZO. They said——?

BRAULIO. They didn't leave us in the dark, you may be sure. It appears Don Lorenzo had an attack the night before last. You know all about it better than we do.

DON LORENZO. [*In a heavy sombre tone.*] Yes.

BENITO. They say he strangled a poor old woman. [*Don Lorenzo recoils in horror, and covers his face with his hands.*]

BRAULIO. There's a fellow for you! A good beginning—that's clear enough. It's always the same thing. The family——

DON LORENZO. The family! [*Removes his hands from his face, walks a few steps as if shaken by an electric shock, and stares at them with keen anxiety, speaking in the same dead voice.*]

BRAULIO. Yes, the family—'tis natural enough.—Don't they say he wanted to give all his fortune away? ever so many millions. The devil of a lunatic altogether. Nothing else for it but what has been decided—to pack him off. We take him away and the poor ladies are left in peace.

DON LORENZO. I!—they?—Ángela?—Inés—no, no—not possible. [*Recoils again R.*]

BRAULIO. [*Staring after him. Aside.*] What's the matter with the gentleman? [*To Benito.*] Look at him, look. [*Both keepers draw together and bend forward in direction R. looking curiously at Don Lorenzo. This group should be made important.*]

DON LORENZO. Air, light! No, not light—darkness! I do not want to see. I do not want to think. [*Falls into arm-chair and lets his head drop into his palms.*]

BENITO. I say, I believe that's——

BRAULIO. This is a fine fix.

BENITO. Who would think it!

BRAULIO. Let us go back to our hiding-place.

BENITO. Sh! Say nothing about it. [*They rise and walk cautiously to the closet, closely watching Don Lorenzo.*]

BRAULIO. That's settled. Not a word. We were told to stay in here. Then let us stay, and we'd have done better not to budge.

BENITO. Somebody is crying and sobbing. [*They reach the door, stand and look at Don Lorenzo, who has not changed his attitude. Servant enters C., crosses and goes out R.*] Leave him alone, leave him alone. Now that he is calm. [*They enter closet and shut door.*]

SCENE X

Don Lorenzo. Dr. Tomás and servant enter R.

DON LORENZO. My God, remove this chalice from my lips—I can endure no more—no more. Oh, strength fails me. [*Sobs despairingly.*] Thou who madest me believe in them. Thou who madest me love them!—and now they—oh, traitors! No, no. Lord who hast given me life, relieve me of its burden soon. See, Lord, how close upon me is the temptation to thrust from me with my

own hands this putrid garb of flesh. To die! How I
yearn for death! Dost thou not see it? See me kneel
to implore it of thee—on my knees. Thou art kind,
thou art compassionate. Death, only death. Send me
death, the pallid messenger of thy love. [*Falls kneeling
beside the arm-chair and drops his head upon folded
arms.*]

DR. TOMÁS. [*In low voice to servant.*] Have they both
come?

SERVANT. [*In same tone to Dr. Tomás.*] Yes, sir; both
the notary and Dr. Bermúdez. [*Dr. Tomás and servant
stand in middle of stage observing Don Lorenzo, who is
kneeling and sobbing.*]

DR. TOMÁS. Poor fellow! [*Steps towards Don Lorenzo,
changes his mind and goes up C.*] Why should I? Let
us make an end of it.

[*Exeunt Dr. Tomás and servant.*]

SCENE XI

Don Lorenzo. Afterwards Dr. Tomás and Dr. Bermúdez.

DON LORENZO. Now am I calmer. The hurt is mortal.
I feel it—here at the heart's core. Thanks, Almighty
consoler. [*Dr. Tomás and Dr. Bermúdez enter C. and
stand watching him.*]

DR. TOMÁS. You see him there—beside the arm-chair.

BERMÚDEZ. Unfortunate man!

DON LORENZO. [*Rising. Aside.*] Ah, miserable being—
still, still—cherishing impossible hopes. Impossible!
And suppose they honestly believe that I——? Oh, but
if they loved me, surely they would not believe it.
[*Despairingly. Pause.*] Did I not hear Inés—the child
I so greatly love—speak of remorse? Why should she
speak of remorse? [*Aloud with increasing agitation.*] All

of them—wretches!—They would almost rejoice at my death. No, then I will not die, no, not until I have fulfilled my duty as an honourable man, not before I have brought the question of my madness to an end.

DR. TOMÁS. [*Placing a hand upon his arm.*] Lorenzo.

DON LORENZO. [*Turning, recognises him, and retreats angrily.*] He!

DR. TOMÁS. Let me introduce one of my best friends, Dr. Bermúdez. [*Pause. Don Lorenzo looks at both strangely.*]

BERMÚDEZ. [*In low voice to Dr. Tomás.*] You can see the effort he is making to control himself. There can be no doubt that he is vaguely conscious of his condition.

DON LORENZO. One of your best friends—one of your best friends——

BERMÚDEZ. [*Aside to Dr. Tomás.*] An idea is escaping him, and he is struggling to retain it.

DON LORENZO. [*Ironically.*] Then if he is one of your best friends, your loyalty will be a guarantee of his.

BERMÚDEZ. [*Aside to Dr. Tomás.*] At last he has found the word, but note the unnatural tones of his voice. [*Aloud.*] I come, Dr. Tomás assures me, to witness a most noble deed.

DON LORENZO. And an act of unworthy treason as well.

DR. TOMÁS. Lorenzo!

BERMÚDEZ. [*Aside to Dr. Tomas.*] Let him say what he likes.

DON LORENZO. And of an exemplary chastisement.

BERMÚDEZ. [*Aside to Dr. Tomas.*] It is very serious, my friend, very serious.

DON LORENZO. [*To Dr. Tomás.*] Call everybody, everybody, my own and strangers alike. Let them come here, and let them await my orders here while I am doing my duty elsewhere. What are you waiting for?

BERMÚDEZ. [*Aside to Dr. Tomás.*] You must not contradict him. Call them. [*Dr. Tomás rings a bell. Enter servant, to whom he speaks in low voice, and then goes out R.*]

DON LORENZO. 'Tis the last test. They almost inspire me with pity, the traitors! Oh, I am well sustained by the certainty of triumph. Be still, my heart. There they are, there they are! I can't see them—I who loved them so fondly. I cannot, and still my eyes turn to them, seeking them, seeking them ever.

SCENE XII

Don Lorenzo, Dr. Tomás and Bermúdez. Doña Ángela. Inés, the Duchess and Edward, R.

DON LORENZO. Inés! It is not possible. She! No, no, it cannot be, my child! [*Goes towards her with outstretched arms. Inés runs to him.*]

INÉS. Father! [*Bermúdez hastens to interpose, and separates them roughly.*]

BERMÚDEZ. Come, come, Don Lorenzo, you might hurt your daughter very seriously.

DON LORENZO. [*Seizing his arm and shaking him violently.*] You scoundrel! Who are you to tear my child away from me?

DR. TOMÁS. Lorenzo!

EDWARD. Don Lorenzo!

DOÑA ÁNGELA. Oh, heavens! [*The ladies group together instinctively. Inés in her mother's arms, the Duchess near them. Dr. Tomás and Edward rush to free Bermúdez of Don Lorenzo's grasp.*]

DON LORENZO. [*Aside, controlling himself.*] So! the imbeciles believe it is another access of madness. Madness! Ha, ha, ha! [*Laughs in a suppressed way. Everybody watches him.*]

BERMÚDEZ. [*Aside to Dr. Tomas.*] It is quite evident.

DOÑA ÁNGELA. [*Aside.*] Oh, my poor husband!

INÉS. [*Aside.*] My father!

DON LORENZO. [*Aside.*] Now they will see how my madness is going to end. Before I leave this house with what a hearty pleasure will I kick that doctor out. Fresh vigour already animates me. What! Since when has it become reason sufficient to declare a man mad because he is resolved to perform his duty? Ah, that's not very likely. Humanity is neither so blind nor so base, though it is bad enough. Softly now. Treason has begun its work; then let the punishment begin too. [*Aloud.*] The hour has come for me to accomplish a sacred obligation, however sharp a sorrow it may be. It were a useless trouble to insist upon your presence at the necessary legal formalities. It would only bore you. The representative of law awaits me in yonder room. I, in obeying a higher law, am about to renounce a fortune that is not mine, as well as a name that neither I nor my family can any longer bear with a clear conscience. Afterwards I will return here, and with my wife and—and—my daughter, will leave this house, which in the past has only sheltered love and felicity, and to-day offers me nothing but treason and wickedness. Let no one seek to prevent me, for none of you can resist my will. Gentlemen [*to Dr. Tomás and Bermúdez*], do me the favour to go before—I beg you. [*All slowly enter closet R. On the threshold Don Lorenzo looks back once at Inés.*]

SCENE XIII

Doña Ángela, Inés, Duchess, and Edward.

The three women in the middle of the stage, Edward listening at the closet door.

INÉS. Oh, pity, Heaven, and save him.

DOÑA ÁNGELA. [*Embracing her.*] You are right. Let us only think of him, pray for him alone.

DUCHESS. It is a sacred duty for you to place poor Don Lorenzo's welfare before your own happiness; but in any case, it is no less a sacred obligation to conform to a higher will than ours. [*Pause.*]

INÉS. [*To Edward.*] What are they saying? Tell us, Edward, what they are saying.

EDWARD. He is talking; his words are cold and severe, but not in the least uncertain or troubled. [*Edward returns to the door.*]

DOÑA ÁNGELA. What anguish! What anxiety! Death were preferable to this torture.

INÉS. What can it matter what my father says since he is already judged beforehand?

DOÑA ÁNGELA. Don't say such a thing, child.

INÉS. I say it because I feel it to be true, and I see it in the faces of those who are now his judges.

DOÑA ÁNGELA. But what—what is it you see?

INÉS. In those persons the monomania of specialists.

DOÑA ÁNGELA. In Tomás?

INÉS. Yes—his scientific opinions—whatever they may be—his own special follies——

DOÑA ÁNGELA. But in me, Inés?

INÉS. [*Embracing her.*] Your love of me.

DOÑA ÁNGELA. Hush, child, hush!

INÉS. They are all against my father, every one. Poor father!

DUCHESS. You are raving, Inés.

INÉS. Yes, I am raving, and so are you, and so are all of us—all excepting him, excepting him—my heart tells me so. You yourself, madam, what is it you desire but Edward's happiness; and Edward wants my love, and I his. My father, with his virtue and his honour, is our mutual obstacle, while in us something obscure twists itself about us till conscience is enveloped in shadows. Oh, my father, my dearest father!

DOÑA ÁNGELA. For pity's sake, Inés! What ideas!

INÉS. What is he saying—tell me what he is saying! I hear his voice.

EDWARD. [*Approaching.*] He is speaking of conclusive evidence.

INÉS. Would to God there were. [*To Edward.*] And now?

EDWARD. They are demanding to see the evidence in order to draw up the act and present it to the judge.

DOÑA ÁNGELA. And he?

EDWARD. He is smiling triumphantly. He is pale, fearfully pale, but composed and dignified. Here they are coming. [*Edward comes down the stage and says aside.*] That man terrifies me.

INÉS. [*Aside.*] God grant it may be true—though my love should perish.

DOÑA ÁNGELA. [*To the Duchess.*] Can it be true?

DUCHESS. [*To Doña Ángela.*] Can it be true?

EDWARD. [*Aside, seeing Don Lorenzo enter.*] Ah, is it I who am mad?

LAST SCENE

Doña Ángela, Inés, the Duchess, Edward, Don Lorenzo, Bermúdez, and Dr. Tomás.

The position of the persons is as follows. The three women form a group at sofa; Edward behind the sofa looking at Don Lorenzo in terror, dominated by him. Don Lorenzo advances to the middle of the stage, with a proud, calm bearing. Behind him come Dr. Tomás and Bermúdez, who remain standing near door C.

DON LORENZO. [*Approaches table, and triumphantly places one hand on desk.*] Here is the proof. Here lies the truth! [*Pause. Opens desk and takes out envelope with blank sheet. Comes down stage. On one side Dr. Tomás and Bermúdez. Edward approaches him on the other.*] Woe to them who think to sacrifice me to their own interests and passions! Bitter will be their deception and most cruel their punishment! Would to God my forgiveness could mitigate it for them. [*Deeply moved.*]

DOÑA ÁNGELA. [*Coming nearer.*] Lorenzo!

INÉS. Father——

DON LORENZO. Here is the proof, Tomás; here is the proof, Ángela, here, my child, is the proof. Listen. [*Pause. Don Lorenzo opens envelope. All gather round him.*] This is—what is this? [*Holds paper away from his eyes, over which he rubs his hand.*] What shade is this that dims my eyes? Can it be that there are tears in them which impede clear vision? No,—I cried before—but now I am not weeping. [*Looks at paper again with horrible anxiety, opens it altogether, and seeks for writing on all sides.*] Where are the words that woman wrote? I have read them a thousand times—and now I can't—— [*To Dr. Tomás, holding out paper to him.*] What does it say?—read, read—quickly—only tell me what it says.

DR. TOMÁS. Nothing, my poor friend.

DON LORENZO. Nothing! [*Again looks at paper.*] You are deceiving me. Dr. Bermúdez, that fellow is deceiving me. He is one of the scoundrels who have plotted this wretched treason. Read it you—read it.

BERMÚDEZ. There is nothing written on the paper.

DON LORENZO. Nothing written on it! You say there is nothing written upon it! It is not true—no, it is not true. Inés, my daughter, my best beloved, come and save your father.—What does it say?

INÉS. Oh, father, I see nothing.

DON LORENZO. Nothing!—she also!—But is this not the proof?

DR. TOMÁS. Yes, my unhappy friend—the proof—but a far too cruel one.

DON LORENZO. [*Striking his forehead.*] Ah, I understand. [*Looks at Dr. Tomás and Doña Ángela.*] I heard them once before talking of a proof. You! [*to Dr. Tomás*] and you! [*To Doña Ángela.*] You have taken it away. God in Heaven! [*Recoils from them in horror. The rest move away from him, and he stands alone in the middle of the stage. Pause.*] Be it so,—be it so!—I am defeated—most miserably defeated! How they rejoice in their triumph! See how they gaze at me in their hypocritical distress! And they feign to weep, too. They are all feigning. [*Pause.*] Alas! my heart—alas! for my life's illusion—alas! for love, and oh, alas! alas! my child—phantoms that whirl about and fly from me—for ever fly away!—I who believed in all things good—in the blue above, in the purity of my daughter's brow—what is there now left me to believe in? You see for yourselves. I make no resistance. I yield myself up. Yours the victory. Why have you brought those men here when I do not seek to oppose your will? I will go wherever you bid me. Adieu. Don't touch me. [*To Dr.*

Tomás, who approaches and takes his hand.] When human flesh comes in contact with mine, it seems to me that vipers crawl along my skin. Alone—alone will I ascend my Calvary bearing my cross of sorrows without an infamous Cyrenean to assist me. Farewell, loyal friend [*still addresses Dr. Tomás*], who have saved the fortune of this disconsolate family from the hands of a madman. Farewell, Ángela, my tender-hearted wife. Twenty years ago, mad with love of you, I gave you my first kiss. To-day, no less a madman, I send you the last. [*Kisses his hand to her with cry and expression of desperate grief.*]

DOÑA ÁNGELA. Lorenzo!

DON LORENZO. Don't come near me. I might strangle you in my arms. [*Ángela recoils.*] Farewell, Inés, my only child. Be happy—if you can. To you I say nothing. I could not speak to you unkindly. [*Walks a few steps feebly, then stops. Repulses roughly those who rush to his assistance.*] Let me be. I require no one. My brow is damp with sweat, and thirst is upon my dry lips, and a fiery heat seems to swell my eyelids. [*Stops again.*] Listen to me, Inés, my child.—If you still retain any love for me,—if by chance your heart is touched with pity for your father,—if you feel regret for what you have done against me along with the rest of them—come once to my arms. Let me carry away into the hell of suffering that awaits me one tear of your eyes upon my cheek, one kiss of your dear lips upon mine.

INÉS. Father! [*All endeavour to restrain her, but she breaks from them and runs to Don Lorenzo, who catches her in his arms and holds her closely clasped to his breast.*]

DON LORENZO. My child! [*The rest advance to them, but make no effort to separate them.*]

INÉS. No—they must not take you away—I love you dearly,—every one lies but you.

Don Lorenzo. You would not have those men carry me off?

Inés. No, no; I will defend you—and you defend me.

Don Lorenzo. Yes! I will defend you—Let them drag you from my arms if they can. [*Makes a movement to carry her away.*]

Doña Ángela. My child, my child! Help! [*Edward, Dr. Tomás and Bermúdez struggle to separate father and daughter.*]

Don Lorenzo. I will not let her go—for ever in my arms!

Inés. Yes, yes, father. Defend me.

Bermúdez. It is imperative.

Edward. Don Lorenzo!

Dr. Tomás. Lorenzo!

Duchess. Merciful god, he will kill her as he killed Juana!

Doña Angela. Inés! [*These exclamations are simultaneous: the struggle is swift. Keepers enter. The men hold Don Lorenzo, and the women restrain Inés, keeping her by force from her father.*]

Edward. At last!

Inés. Father! [*Holds her arms out to Don Lorenzo.*]

Don Lorenzo. I was not able, child.—I could do no more.—Here upon my cheek I feel your kisses and your tears.—She at least loved me—she was innocent—I see it now. God above, thou hast accepted my martyrdom in that night of agony and temptation in exchange for her happiness. I do not regret it. Make her happy—very happy! and let the cup of bitterness be mine alone—only mine!

Inés. Adieu, father—I will save you yet.

Don Lorenzo. What can you do, child—when God himself has not seen fit to save me? [*Remains near closet between keepers, guarded by Edward, Dr. Tomás and Bermúdez. Inés, held back by the other women, stands with arms strained towards him.*]

Curtain

www.ingramcontent.com/pod-product-compliance
Lightning Source LLC
Chambersburg PA
CBHW011341090426
42743CB00018B/3405